The Monocle Book of Designers on Sofas

MONOCLE

First published in the United Kingdom in 2025
by MONOCLE and Thames & Hudson Ltd,
6—24 Britannia Street, London WC1X 9JD
thamesandhudson.com

First published in the United States of America in 2025
by MONOCLE and Thames & Hudson Inc,
500 Fifth Avenue, New York, New York, 10110
thamesandhudsonusa.com

MONOCLE is a trading name of Winkontent Limited

© 2025 Winkontent Limited of Midori House,
1 Dorset Street, London W1U 4EG

EU Authorized Representative: Interart S.A.R.L.
19 rue Charles Auray, 93500 Pantin, Paris, France
productsafety@thameshudson.co.uk
interart.fr

British Library Cataloguing-in-Publication Data
A catalogue record for this book is available from
The British Library

Library of Congress Control Number: 2025934118

For more information, please visit *monocle.com*

MIX
Paper | Supporting
responsible forestry
FSC
www.fsc.org
FSC® C013123

This book was printed on paper certified
according to the standards of the FSC®

Edited by *Nic Monisse* and *Virginia McLeod*
Designed by *Monocle*
Typeset in *Plantin* and *Helvetica Neue*
Printed in *Italy* by *Graphicom*

ISBN 978-0-500-96642-6
01

The
Monocle
Book of
Designers
on Sofas

M

T&H

Contents

006   Take a seat
      Nic Monisse

Chapter 01.

Profiles of 50 designers on their sofas

010   David Caon & Jeramie Hotz
      on the Maralunga sofa

014   Bjarke Ingels
      on the Brick sofa

018   Gabriel Tan & Cherie Er
      on the Luva sofa

022   Marcio Kogan
      on the Horizonte sofa

024   Ini Archibong
      on the Anagram sofa

028   Amale Andraos & Dan Wood
      on the Polder sofa

032   Brigitte Shim
      on a custom-made window seat

036   Patricia Urquiola
      on the Dudet Bold sofa

038   John Wardle
      on the Gentry sofa

042   Sabine Marcelis & Paul Cournet
      on the Lisse sofa

046   Joris Poggioli
      on the Patrick sofa

048   Betty Ng
      on the Marenco sofa

052   Farshid Moussavi
      on the Osaka sofa

056   Eran Chen
      on the Extrasoft sofa

060   Yinka Ilori
      on a custom-upcycled sofa

062   Steven Holl & Dimitra Tsachrelia
      on the Club sofa

066   Nada Debs
      on the Zen sofa

070   Jay Osgerby
      on the Elan sofa

074   Naoto Fukasawa
      on the Hiroshima sofa

076   Yuichi Kodai & Claudia Maggi
      on the Sumo sofa

080   Ilse Crawford
      on the Ilse sofa

084   Angie Brooks & Lawrence Scarpa
      on a custom-made sofa

088   Tosin Oshinowo
      on the Aidan sofa

090   Jasper Morrison
      on the Jota sofa

094   Rodrigo Bravo
      on the Can sofa

098   Eric Owen Moss
      on the Theatre sofa

102   Daniel Libeskind
      on the Big C sofa

106   Yuko Nagayama
      on the Sax sofa

108 Tatiana Bilbao
on the Soft Dream sofa

112 Keiji Ashizawa
on the A-So1 sofa

116 Thomas Hildebrand
on the DS-80 daybed

120 Nifemi Marcus-Bello
on the Äpplaryd sofa

124 Rahul Mehrotra
on the Correa sofa

126 Mariam Issoufou
on the Strato sofa

130 Chatpong Chuenrudeemol
on a custom-made sofa

134 David Thulstrup & Martin Nielsen
on the Karm sofa

138 Hunn Wai & Olivia Lee
on the Söderhamn sofa

140 David Welsh & Chris Major
on the 801 Series sofa

144 Fien Muller & Hannes Van Severen
on the Pillow sofa

146 Niall & Helen Maxwell
on the FD147L sofa

150 Fernanda Canales
on the Siesta sofa

154 Sigurd Larsen
on the A Sofa

156 Tamsin Johnson
on a custom-made sofa

160 Dorte Mandrup
on the Poet sofa

164 Joyce Wang
on a custom-made sofa

166 Federica Biasi & Moreno Vannini
on the Niveaux sofa

170 Ronan Bouroullec
on the Slow sofa

174 Alfredo Paredes
on the Santana sofa

178 Grant Wilkinson & Teresa Rivera
on the Peonia sofa

180 Alex Mustonen & Anita Maritz
on the Sunday sofa

Chapter 02.

The history of the sofa

186 The sofa: a brief history
Stella Roos

192 A century (and a quarter)
of sofa design
Virginia McLeod

196 100 sofas:
An illustrated chronology

216 Directory of designers

218 Directory of sofas

220 Index

222 Acknowledgements

223 About Monocle

Take a seat
Nic Monisse

The sofa is by many measures the most important piece of furniture that one can own. Often, it is the most expensive item in a home or office; frequently, it's also the largest and allows multiple people to sit together, fostering connection. Such traits make it a significant, personality-defining object, with its form and materiality contributing to a space's atmosphere, from minimalist to playful. All of this combines to create a piece of furniture that people tend to hang onto. Over years of use, a settee accumulates memories, from family milestones and quiet evenings to lively gatherings. As such, they speak volumes about our personalities and lifestyles. The creatives who have let us into their homes and workplaces in this book tell this tale beautifully.

One's choice of sofa says a lot about one's chosen mode of living. For designers and architects, there is an added layer of meaning: their professional lives mean the choice of perch can reflect their core design philosophies.

Take Mexican architect Fernanda Canales' bespoke sofa, nicknamed "Siesta", which she describes as a "non-design" object. It is a piece of furniture that doesn't seek to define the space it's in, directly embodying her ethos of creating flexible environments. This outlook shouldn't come as a surprise for a piece of furniture that naturally facilitates different activities. Switzerland-based Nigerian-American designer Ini Archibong uses his Vitra sofa as a workspace, playground and cinema. London-based Jay Osgerby's Elan even served as a delivery table for his child's birth.

The sofa, it seems, is both a silent witness and supportive participant in family and work life. For Hong Kong-based Betty Ng, the purchase of an Arflex Marenco sofa – her first "serious" sofa after years of making do in rented spaces – became a symbol of being able to settle down.

Similarly, for Danish designer David Thulstrup, the selection of his own Karm sofa for his renovated childhood home, after years abroad, represented his choice to put down roots. It reshaped the space, much like Daniel Libeskind's decision to integrate an enormous Pierre Paulin-designed sofa into his compact Manhattan apartment. Its addition prompted a rethinking of his furniture, which had the effect of "a major renovation". It's safe to say that the piece will be there for the long haul – and it's a choice that Libeskind is happy with, explaining that the sofa in question also functions as a sculpture, sitting at the intersection of design and art.

London-based design duo Grant Wilkinson and Teresa Rivera see the sofa that they designed for their home in a similar light. Like much of their work, the Peonia sofa appears to be in motion due to its sculptural, wavy aesthetics, adding a sense of play to their living room. Meanwhile, Danish architect Bjarke Ingels' Brick sofa is a sculptural interpretation of sandbags, stacked in a manner that remains visually appealing from all sides.

It's clear that the sofa is more than just a place to take a seat. Indeed, it often reveals deeper cultural connections. Japanese architect Keiji Ashizawa, designer of the A-SOI sofa, created it to reflect Japanese *tatami* culture (in which people sit, eat and socialise from the floor). Meanwhile, Thai architect Chatpong Chuenrudeemol's custom, built-in sofa at his home in Bangkok – which serves as a couch, workbench and family meeting point – reflects the need for furniture and architecture to do many things at once in dense Southeast Asian cities.

Such cultural factors also reflect the personal attachments that we have to the sofa. And for good reason: these pieces stay with us for extended periods, with strong emotional associations formed over decades. Australian architects David Welsh and Chris Major refer to their 23-year-old Woodmark sofa as "the hearth of the house", a resilient fixture that has "seen many wars" through years of children, dogs and family gatherings. Similarly, Mexican architect Tatiana Bilbao hopes that her Soft Dream sofa by Flexform – over a decade old and well used – will eventually be passed down to her children.

While they are often the largest item in a room, the sofa also plays a large role in our lives. With this in mind, join us as we visit the homes of leading creatives to hear about their settees. Get comfy, read on and don't forget to plump the cushions when you're done.

Nic Monisse is Monocle's *design editor. He also hosts* Monocle on Design, *a weekly 30-minute radio programme showcasing the best in the world of design, craft and graphics. A landscape architect by training, the Australian-born journalist has reported on stories across the globe.*

Chapter 01.

Designers on Sofas

Profiles of 50 designers on their sofas

David Caon &
Jeramie Hotz
On the
Maralunga sofa

Sydney, Australia

David Caon and Jeramie Hotz's home is a testament to mid-century Italian design. Their two-and-a-half-seater Maralunga has become a well-loved fixture, adapting to the family's changing lifestyle – embodying their belief in design's ability to evolve with its owners.

JOE COLOMBO
Poltrona Frau

Sofa designer
Vico Magistretti

Manufacturer
Cassina

Year designed
1973

About the sofa
The Maralunga sofa, designed by Italian architect Vico Magistretti in 1973 for Cassina, is a celebrated icon of modern furniture design (*see page 208*). Renowned for its innovative blend of comfort and functionality, the sofa features a unique adjustable headrest mechanism, allowing users to switch between a low or high backrest with a gentle pull – a design element inspired by a bicycle chain. This feature was revolutionary at the time, marrying casual elegance with ergonomic versatility.

About the owners
Partners in work and in life, industrial designer David Caon and studio director Jeramie Hotz lead Caon Design Office, a Sydney-based studio renowned for its diverse portfolio, from aircraft interiors for Australia's flagship airline Qantas to workspace furniture, as well as bespoke projects. The duo's work is deeply rooted in the human experience, spanning contexts and disciplines as varied as product, interior and transportation design.

David Caon is renowned for his forward-thinking, future-facing industrial design. But at home with his wife and collaborator Jeramie Hotz, his eyes are firmly set on the past. "Our space is a bit of a homage to late mid-century Italian, my favourite era of design," says Caon. "It's all pretty classic – that kind of bulletproof design."

Some of it, however, is certainly not child-proof. When Caon and Hotz had a son, then a daughter, their tribute to Italian design became the backdrop for play. The kids don't know (or care) that they're weaving around a Gae Aulenti coffee table, illuminated by

"A special sofa needs to be a bit unusual, something that you don't see every day – something that's not too perfect"

Joe Colombo lamps and Achille Castiglioni Flos lighting. And they definitely don't grasp the eminence of the family's two-and-a-half-seat Vico Magistretti-designed Maralunga sofa by Cassina, which they've annexed for themselves. "We've already had it reupholstered once but we'll need to do it again," says Caon. "Luckily it's nice and dark so we can get away with pen marks that the kids have left." The couple's border terrier, Peaches, is also a Magistretti aficionado and her lounging restricts the couple's sofa time even further.

But Caon and Hotz ultimately have their children to thank for the sofa's acquisition. Prior to expanding their family, two Walter Knoll chairs, with fragile black-velvet upholstering, were the pride of Caon's collection. "And then we got ourselves a little baby and I thought, 'These won't survive,'" says Caon.

So the chairs were rehomed, at the same time as a friend's well-loved Maralunga auspiciously became available to them. "That was the genesis of getting the sofa," adds Caon. "The opportunity to acquire it and the need to get rid of something that wouldn't survive the children."

The pair had long coveted a Maralunga – particularly a two-and-half-seat one, which Caon believes to be the truest expression of Magistretti's intent. "Every sofa is extrapolated over different dimensions and seating options, but they don't always translate, and there's always one size that by far looks the best," he says. For Hotz, a standout sofa must be distinctive and idiosyncratic. "A special sofa needs to be a bit unusual, something that you don't see every day – something that's not too perfect," she says. The Maralunga delivers on that front – its signature adjustable backrest, which Caon confesses is not entirely practical, is a feature that they both respect. "It's very charming and endearing, and it probably wouldn't have had the same success without it," he says.

Caon and Hotz received the sofa in original, well-loved condition. Naturally, their first move was to reupholster it – being careful to preserve the Cassina labels and lining – with a verdant Kvadrat fabric. To them, it's part of the fun of vintage furniture. "Vintage sofas can continue to evolve with you," says Caon. "If they're a quality item, they can have a really long life and you can change them as your ideas around how your room should look evolve."

Indeed, the room (and sofa) might need to change again because the children are still stress-testing the sofa's – and the home's – longevity. "We're in a phase where we have to let go," says Caon, reflecting on how long he'll hold out on the sofa's current upholstery. "The house isn't a beautiful, curated design experience – it's more like an exercise in arranging things and hoping they don't get destroyed."

02.
Bjarke Ingels
On the Brick sofa

Copenhagen, Denmark

For Bjarke Ingels, life on Copenhagen's harbour has shaped his design ethos. This is reflected in his home, a reimagined ferry, and its Brick sofas, which are partly inspired by sandbags. These pieces are utilitarian yet sculptural and make for a comfortable seat too.

Sofa designer
KiBiSi

Manufacturer
Jot Jot

Year designed
2010

About the sofa

Designed by Copenhagen-based KiBiSi – a collective composed of designer Lars Holme Larsen of Kilo Design, architect Bjarke Ingels of BIG and brand consultant Jens Martin Skibsted of Skibsted Ideation – the Brick sofa is an exercise in architectural upholstery. Created for Lithuanian firm Jot Jot, it draws inspiration from classic brick-bond patterns. Featuring an arrangement of connected cushions, secured with distinctive concrete buttons and rope, the design has a structural honesty that lends it an industrial aesthetic.

About the owner

Bjarke Ingels, educated at the Royal Danish Academy of Fine Arts, is the founder of Bjarke Ingels Group (BIG). Established in 2005, the design and architecture studio has offices across the globe and is celebrated for championing "hedonistic sustainability" – creating architecture that is both environmentally conscious and immensely enjoyable. The practice is renowned for integrating public space and playful elements into its projects. Portfolio highlights include Copenhagen's CopenHill, a waste-to-energy plant with a ski slope on its roof, and New York's Via 57 West – a hybrid of the European perimeter block building and the traditional American high-rise.

The rise of Danish architect Bjarke Ingels's design practice mirrors the revival of Copenhagen's harbour. "My journey as a practising architect ended up fully coinciding with the rediscovery of the harbour," says Ingels, whose connection with his hometown's waterfront is reflected in his choice of home – a houseboat – and his sofa, which resembles a stack of sandbags used to prevent flooding.

Even when he was a student architect the harbour was front and centre in his life. The designer attended the Royal Danish Academy of Fine Arts in Copenhagen's portside Holmen district – a former military base that was active at the time of his study. "Back then, the school moved out to Holmen and we had to show our student cards to a military guard in order to be let into the premises," says Ingels.

"The idea of the Brick sofa is that it is just layers of pillows – two for the seat, two more for the back. That's it. It has a straightforwardness"

The relationship with the port continued into his practice: Ingels's first commission with his studio Bjarke Ingels Group (BIG) was the revival of the Copenhagen Harbour Baths. "It was 2001 and we had four months and a €520,000 budget – so it was a feverish thing that got whipped out," says Ingels. "But in that sense, our journey has been somehow related to this rise of the port as an important

space in the city. Our own office is now at the tip of the pier."

It's appropriate that his home is on the harbour too. A 38-metre-long decommissioned ferry called *Bukken Bruse* has been entirely reimagined. The roof boasts a sprawling terrace, while the funnels and navigation bridges have been converted into a glass-enclosed pavilion for the main bedroom. Outdoor terraces frame the living space, which was originally a car deck that accommodated four vehicles side by side. Now the living space is dominated by two iterations of the Brick sofa, designed by KiBiSi, the industrial design group that Ingels runs with his two friends Jens Martin Skibsted and Lars Holme Larsen.

"When designing it, we asked the question: what is the sofa, really? It is essentially a pile of pillows for maximum comfort," says Ingels. "These are almost like sandbags – resilience fortification to protect against incoming floods." The trio took that simple idea ("almost without any design", according to Ingels) and extrapolated it into a sofa. Piles of pillows are held in place with Chesterfield-like fibre-concrete buttons and are bound by mountain climbing rope.

"I like it when things look special because they perform specially," says Ingels of the aesthetic of the sofa. "The idea of the Brick sofa is that it is just layers of pillows – two for the seat, two for the back. That's it. It has a straightforwardness." But, importantly, the sofas – an L-shaped lounger and a three-seater – also serve the space. The sculptural quality of the pillows give the loungers a visual appeal when looked at from both the front and the back. "The utilitarian element means that the sofa sits comfortably in the middle of the space without looking like it turns its back," says Ingels. Instead, viewers are invited to enjoy views of the sofa – and the harbour beyond – from every angle.

03.
Gabriel Tan
& Cherie Er
On the Luva sofa

Porto, Portugal

Born from a search for comfort amid an intercontinental move, Gabriel Tan's Luva sofa – or "glove" in Portuguese – extends a metaphorical welcoming hand. It blends familiar forms into a modular design and has become a place for play, reading and connection.

Sofa designer
Gabriel Tan

Manufacturer
Herman Miller

Year designed
2020

About the sofa
The Luva sofa is designed so that it can take multiple forms. It can contract inwards for a supportive, more upright posture or unfold for a more relaxed, reclined position. The design also draws inspiration from the delicate rolled edges, known as *shikibuton*, of Japanese futon mattresses. The resulting curves give the Luva an aesthetic that is both inviting and sophisticated. Luva offers multiple configurations, including armchairs, chaises and multi-section sofas.

About the owner
Industrial designer Gabriel Tan and his partner in business and life, Cherie Er, work at cultural intersections and across disciplines, finding ways to combine tradition and technology, heritage and cosmopolitan aesthetics. The duo's craft-driven design brand, Origin Made, has a studio in Porto. The result is a portfolio of work that reflects their Asian heritage and a knowledge of, and passion for, European design traditions.

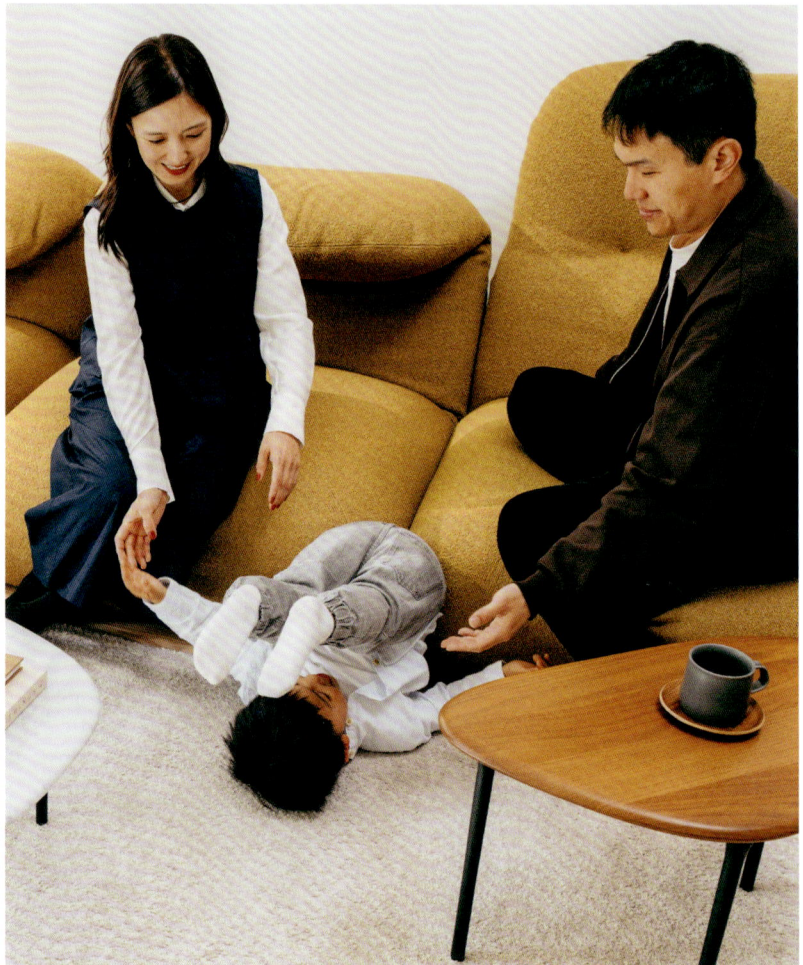

Gabriel Tan's sofa, Luva, takes its name from the Portuguese word for "glove". But in 2020, when he relocated to Porto from Singapore with his wife, Cherie Er, the new country didn't exactly feel like a perfectly snug fit. "It was a very uncomfortable period, emotionally and psychologically," recalls the designer, who is best known for his work as the creative director of Japanese brand Ariake, and the founder (with Er) of Portuguese furniture marque Origin Made.

Not only did Tan, Er and their young family have to contend with pandemic lockdowns on an entirely new continent, they were also living in a rented apartment with unfamiliar furniture, as their new family home hadn't been completed. "I was longing for comfort and security," says Tan. During that winter, the designer began thinking about devising a sofa for their new digs. To do so, he reflected on familiar forms, such as the traditional Japanese futon and the leather boxing glove, as well as an old La-Z-Boy-style chair that his father had owned. "The

"The Luva is like a little obstacle course for the children because of the little humps"

La-Z-Boy was really comfortable but super ugly," says Tan, laughing. "I wanted to make something that was beautiful but had the high-back comfort of that chair – I wanted to better the sofa of my father."

Despite running his own furniture firm, Tan hadn't yet designed a sofa. The pandemic, however, afforded him time to work on such a project – and his life in Porto presented him with a new urban environment full of inspiration. The designer chose to create a modular and easy-to-disassemble sofa, since most apartments in Portugal are compact and are rarely serviced by anything larger than a modest elevator. The result was Luva, which also reflected his desire to give the sofa's owners the opportunity to easily shift the couch out of a living room and into a bedroom, to make more room for events such as house parties or big family gatherings. "I was thinking of the home as a hybrid space, which you can reconfigure," says Tan. "This sofa allows you to do that."

Designed without any formal commission (and not an exact fit for Origin Made), Tan felt some degree of trepidation when sharing his designs for Luva with other creative directors who he hoped might help him to put it into production. Fortunately, Noah Schwarz – vice-president of product design at Herman Miller – appreciated the work. "He said, 'OK, we're currently looking for a new sofa and this checks all the boxes,'" says Tan. "Herman Miller is a very big brand, so it doesn't usually take proposals like this. It was real serendipity."

Despite designing the sofa with his own home in mind, there was no guarantee that once it went to commercial production it would end up in Tan's house. Thankfully, Herman Miller photographed promotional images for the Luva in the designer's townhouse; once the shoot was done, he got to keep the sofa and now it has very much become part of the family. Though it's only a three-seater, it can comfortably accommodate six – more than enough for his household. "It's me, my wife, my mother-in-law and my kids," says Tan. "We don't have a TV, so we sit on the sofa, play and read. The Luva is like a little obstacle course for the children because of the little humps. They probably use it much more than me."

04.
Marcio Kogan
On the Horizonte sofa

São Paulo, Brazil

For many, designing one's own dream sofa, then having it put into production, lies well and truly beyond reach. Not so for Marcio Kogan. The esteemed Brazilian architect's perch of choice is the Horizonte seating system that his firm, Studio MK27, developed in partnership with Italian furniture powerhouse Minotti. "I'm an architect and in my studio, we design everything for our projects," says Kogan, who founded the São Paulo-based practice in the late 1970s. "One day, Minotti called us and asked about our vision for our projects, including the furniture," says Kogan. "I explained that we love to control everything inside a project because we have an obsession for perfection."

It was a conversation that would change the course of work for both Studio MK27 and the Italian furniture company. After the Minotti family visited Brazil they invited Kogan and his team to design for them – to continue that pursuit of perfection. In 2018 the two companies began releasing furniture in partnership, producing the Horizonte collection in 2022.

"It's a Brazilian name, meaning 'horizon'," says Kogan of the sofa, which per its moniker has a low, long and clean-lined form. The architect has used the sofa in MK27 projects, including a sleek apartment in São Paulo (*pictured*), and has picked it for his own home, which is under construction. "I'm choosing it for my apartment because I like its proportions – and I like this bouclé

fabric," he adds, laughing while acknowledging that a white sofa is a bold move. Still, the colour won't stop Kogan from using the lounge; at the weekend he'll be joined by friends and when he's alone, he will be found reading or listening to music on the Horizonte. All of these activities, he says, are enhanced by the fact that the sofa is comfortable enough to spend extended periods of time on. "For a sofa, comfort is the most important thing," says Kogan. "What I love about working with Minotti on Horizonte is that the quality of the finish is perfect. We have a good design and good comfort."

Sofa designer
Studio MK27

Manufacturer
Minotti

Year designed
2022

About the sofa
The Horizonte sofa was designed by Studio MK27, the firm of Brazilian architect Marcio Kogan. It is a modular system that includes side tables, pouffes and L-shaped corner sets. The Horizonte's generously proportioned cushions rest on a simple leather or fabric base, that itself sits on a recessed plinth in matte-black varnished metal, making it appear as though the sofa is suspended in mid-air.

About the owner
Brazilian architect Marcio Kogan graduated from Mackenzie Presbyterian University in São Paulo and explored film-making before establishing Studio MK27 in the late 1970s. The practice has a portfolio defined by pure forms, the use of natural materials such as wood and seamless indoor-outdoor transitions. Key projects include the Paraty House, a striking concrete-and-timber beach house on Brazil's Costa Verde, and the Cultura bookshop-cum-meeting place in São Paulo.

05.
Ini Archibong
*On the
Anagram sofa*

Neuchâtel,
Switzerland

Between travel, parenting and
managing a kaleidoscopic home
mirroring his boundary-pushing
designs, Ini Archibong's work
and home life defy convention.
Offering balance is his modular
Anagram sofa – a grounding
element where creativity and
family life unfold.

Sofa designer
Panter&Tourron

Manufacturer
Vitra

Year produced
2024

About the sofa
Produced by Swiss furniture firm Vitra, the Anagram sofa was created by Franco-Italian studio Panter&Tourron as part of a modular collection built around a versatile base platform module. Backrests and armrest elements can be freely added, allowing for endless configurations from intimate nooks to expansive lounges. Its pillowy comfort stems from polyurethane foam cubes, supported by an internal webbed aluminium frame. Designed for flexibility, the Anagram offers optional attachable side tables and features removable covers, embodying a thoughtful blend of adaptability and comfort.

About the owner
Born in California to Nigerian parents, Ini Archibong blends his multicultural upbringing with a rigorous education from ArtCenter College of Design in Los Angeles and Switzerland's ÉCAL. His approach to design is influenced by a unique blend of mythology, spirituality and craftsmanship, creating pieces that inspire wonder and tell profound stories. Archibong's creations can be found in prestigious collections, including the National Museum of African American History and Culture, Dallas Museum of Art and The Metropolitan Museum of Art, alongside collaborations with brands such as Hermès and Sé.

"I don't have a typical life," says Ini Archibong. "I'm on the road constantly and I'm a single dad, so everything in my home is geared around efficiency and creativity." This atypical approach to the day-to-day shouldn't come as a surprise: the Swiss-based, Nigerian-American industrial designer's work is known for breaking the mould.

Headline grabbing and boundary pushing commissions include a sound-emitting egg sculpture created with Japanese craftsmen, rock-like furniture with its own drainage system, hand-carved glass pendants and even packaging for Snoop Dogg and Dr Dre's Gin & Juice drink. It's a body of work that is naturally reflected in Archibong's home in Neuchâtel, where a kaleidoscope of colour and objects occupy the space. And it's among these accoutrements that an Anagram sofa by Vitra takes pride of place.

"Since I moved to Switzerland, Vitra's been the go-to for me," says Archibong. "One of my chairs is in the Vitra Museum's permanent collection and I've been taking my daughter there since she was born – she thinks of it as a playground." In addition to having a connection with the brand, Archibong has a close relationship with the two designers behind the Anagram, Stefano Panterotto and Alexis Tourron. The duo run Lausanne-based Panter&Tourron and were former classmates of Archibong's at ÉCAL – the university of art and design in Lausanne. "My flat is full of my own stuff, so it feels great to have pieces designed by friends, colleagues and people I look up to like Stefano and Alexis," says Archibong. "It's nice to watch the development of each other's projects and to have that story behind the pieces."

This attachment to story should be expected from Archibong, whose work is frequently rooted in heritage and craft traditions, while also drawing inspiration from narrative storytelling, including film and comics. "Most of the things in my home were collected as my daughter grew up," says the designer. "The year she was born, all I really had was a computer, a Togo chair, a mattress, a TV, two spoons, two forks, two coffee mugs and two crystal Saint-Louis glasses. Now I have every little seashell she has brought me, Murano glass figurines, fantastical prototypes of things I've made for collectors and almost

> "It's the grounding element for the home. While everything else might disappear into another universe, the sofa is very real"

all the art I wish I had as a teenager, from artists like Hebru Brantley. The whole flat is a giant fantasy land that fuels our creativity."

It's a creativity supported by the sofa. Its slender aluminium frame and deep, inviting cushions are modular; there's also a complementary attachable table, which Archibong uses to facilitate different activities. "It's so comfortable that it's almost the most used piece of furniture in my home," he says. "I should be doing my sketching in the studio but I do it on the sofa with an attachable table," he adds, adding that he can often be found reclining while watching movies or spread out on its cushions, playing with his daughter (jumping on the sofa is permitted if the cashmere blankets and Hermès pillows have been removed). In short, it's a stable platform upon which the lives of Archibong and his daughter play out.

06.
Amale Andraos
& Dan Wood
On the Polder sofa

Rhode Island,
USA

In Amale Andraos and Dan
Wood's Rhode Island home,
architectural vision is balanced
with domestic reality. Here,
the duo's prized Polder sofa
commands the room's finest view,
with the whole family – including
Luna the dog – fighting to get
the best seat in the house.

Sofa designer
Hella Jongerius

Manufacturer
Vitra

Year designed
2005

About the sofa
Dutch designer Hella Jongerius devised this modular system consisting of irregularly-sized cushions and couch elements. The upholstery of every element is a different hue of a single colour, creating a subtle patchwork. This varied effect is reminiscent of stretches of fields in the Netherlands that have been reclaimed from the sea with dykes and drainage canals; the sofa takes its name from the Dutch word for those low-lying flatlands. Its decorative buttons are made from natural materials including buffalo horn, olive wood and bamboo. These are cross-stitched into the cushions to give a handcrafted feel.

About the owners
Lebanese-born Amale Andraos is a professor and former dean at Columbia University and US-born Dan Wood is a fellow of the American Institute of Architects. Together they run WorkAC, a New York-based design studio founded in 2003 and celebrated for integrating architecture, urbanism and landscape to create unexpected, sustainable interventions. Portfolio highlights include the North Boulder Library, the Rhode Island School of Design Student Success Center and the Museum Garage in Miami, where a parking garage was combined with a vertical public space.

Amale Andraos and Dan Wood are the principals of New York architecture firm WorkAC, which they founded together in 2003. But Andraos and Wood are partners in more than one sense, having been married since 2001. The duo's global portfolio of projects focuses on structures with a civic purpose, including libraries, institutional buildings and art museums. It also includes the Riverhouse, a home that they designed for their family in Rhode Island. "This house is an experiment," says Wood. "It's a chance to do everything we've always wanted to do, all in one project. That logic extended to the furniture. It's filled with pieces we wanted to live with."

One such piece is a Polder sofa, designed by Netherlands-born Hella Jongerius and produced by Vitra, which takes pride of place in the living room. One of the reasons why Andraos and Wood were attracted to the sofa is that it evokes the golden era of late 1990s Dutch design, which saw designers such as Marcel Wanders, Richard Hutten and Gijs Bakker rise to prominence alongside architecture firms such as OMA. The couple lived in Rotterdam during that period, experiencing the scene first-hand and discovering the work of Jongerius in the process. "It has a look that is really of that moment, when architecture firms were opening in Rotterdam every week," says Wood of the sofa, with Andraos adding that its aesthetic captures the period's sense of adventure. "It has this really interesting aesthetic that's both modern and postmodern at the same time," she says. "It is serious while being funny."

In the Riverhouse, the Polder sofa anchors a large, multi-functional open space. "It faces very big windows looking out onto the landscape and a river," says Wood. "It's the best view in the house." It's a position that means the couch is a popular perch for the creative duo and their two children. It is also coveted by the family dog, Luna, who is not allowed to sit on the Polder – at least in principle. "Luna sneaks onto our couches at night when we're all asleep," says Andraos. "Dan creates barricades to keep her off but then the rest of us can't use the sofa the next morning. Luna's allowed everywhere else, including our bed; the sofa is a red line but one that she crosses all the time."

"It's a memory of our early days in Rotterdam, so there's an element of connection with it"

Despite the sofa playing an important role in their home life – and the duo working on countless furniture designs for their own projects – neither Andraos nor Wood has designed a sofa. Wood suggests this is due in part to both design contracts and his own tastes. "Furniture such as banquettes are included in the architecture budget, while sofas are part of the interior-design budget," he says. "Plus, if you forced me to choose a chair or a sofa, my tendency would be to pick a chair. I'm always a little more comfortable in a chair, though I'll definitely sleep on a sofa."

But should such a brief come their way, they would be prepared. "The most important aspect of a sofa is proportion," says Andraos. "Proportion can lead to comfort but the two are not always related." It is a balance, however, that the Polder strikes.

07.
Brigitte Shim
On a custom-made window seat

Toronto, Canada

Brigitte Shim sees sofas as extensions of her architecture. At the Ace Hotel in Toronto, rather than rely on stand-alone pieces, she carved sofas into the building itself. It's an approach that creates unique vantage points and blurs divisions between the interior and the city beyond.

Sofa designer
Shim-Sutcliffe

Manufacturer
Custom installation

Year designed
2022

About the sofa
Shim-Sutcliffe's handsome, red-brick tower for the Ace Hotel's first outpost in Canada includes 123 guest rooms, each of whose large picture windows are framed with a window seat, conceived as a comfortable nook within each bedroom. These sofas are made from materials that evoke simplicity – plywood frames echo the canvas-lined bedroom walls and the exposed concrete of the ceilings. The leather upholstery was chosen for its comfort, its durability and for the fact that its patina changes with use.

About the owner
Brigitte Shim co-founded Toronto's Shim-Sutcliffe Architects with Howard Sutcliffe in 1994. The studio is celebrated for an architectural ethos that has reshaped cities across the globe, encouraging people to reconsider how urban environments can become more efficient and to embrace the special characteristics of their locale and immediate microclimates. Key projects include The Integral House in Toronto – a sinuous concrete-and-wood dwelling nestled in a ravine – and their own home, the Laneway House, which ingeniously maximises space on a narrow urban lot.

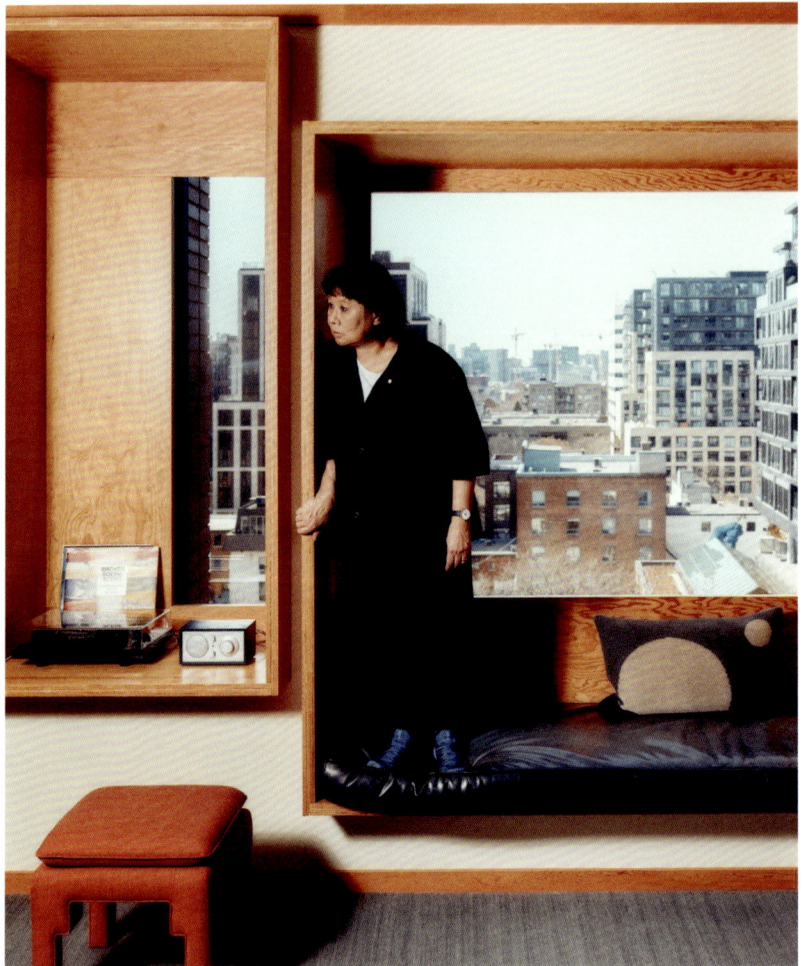

When Brigitte Shim says that she and her husband, Howard Sutcliffe, do not own a sofa, that is not entirely true. "I guess the way that we tend to think about sofas is that they're literally carved into the architecture," says Shim, who co-founded Canadian architecture studio Shim-Sutcliffe with Sutcliffe in 1994. "The idea is that the sofa isn't just a piece of furniture. It's actually a piece of the building and it connects to the heart and soul of the space."

So, while the living room at their home in Toronto – the award-winning Laneway House, which they built in the early 1990s – is furnished with an array of standalone chairs

"When you're in the zone of the window sofa, you're not quite in the city but you're also not in your room either"

that the pair have collected over the years (a mix of heritage pieces acquired during their travels, family heirlooms and a bespoke edition of the HAB lounge chair that the pair designed in 2004 for Canadian furniture manufacturer Nienkämper), their approach to designing sofas is often an integral part of the architectural process. In short, it's less about standalone pieces and more about the integration of furniture and architecture.

"A sofa can make unique vantage points," says Shim. "It creates these kinds of cosy corners – you might be at one end of the sofa, looking out, or you're in the middle taking in a different portion of the room. So, the view from the sofa really becomes a key aspect of what makes a room successful. It is literally a part of how you shape a space."

The pair have woven that approach into their studio's designs – both for private clients and for themselves – over the years. Shim says that a favourite perch is at Toronto's Ace Hotel (*pictured*), which opened in 2022, where they framed large picture-windows in each of the guest rooms with a warm, plywood and leather window seat. Conceived as a nook within the bedroom, it is a space where the hotel room's interior and the cityscape outside appear to converge.

"We thought of the window seats at the Ace as a threshold of sorts," says Shim. "So, when you're in the zone of the window-sofa, you're not quite in the city but you're also not in your room either. You're in this in-between space, which is anchored by the sofa, and it becomes a pretty unique vantage point."

From these window seats, Shim says that you can sit and look out over the park or into the city. But, she adds, they have also been designed for internal reflection too: the lighting by the seat can be directed up at the wood ceiling to create an ambient light or turned around and pointed downwards, becoming a reading lamp. "So the sofa allows you to do a few different things when you're in that space," says Shim. "We really wanted to build that into the design."

To further its versatility, Shim says that the sofa was upholstered in leather, due to the material's durability, comfort and the patina that it accrues with time and use. The result is a hardwearing and flexible form that encapsulates the approach to sofa design that Shim-Sutcliffe has honed throughout its existence. "A sofa has so many lives," says Shim. "It can do many things for you at different times of the day and that is what makes it really key to a space."

08.
Patricia Urquiola
On the Dudet Bold sofa

Milan, Italy

For Spanish architect and designer Patricia Urquiola, a sofa is a landscape. "It's more than just a piece of furniture," she says. "It's an island for living." The one in her home is her own creation, made for Italian furniture firm Cassina, for whom she is art director. Called the Dudet Bold sofa, it is a continuation of the armchair of the same name and follows its simple yet playful spirit. "Sometimes, certain design intuitions stay with you – they ask to be explored," says Urquiola. "The Dudet Bold sofa takes the armchair's original intuition and amplifies it: more volume, more presence, more generosity, almost like a magnified version of itself."

Inspired by the silhouettes of the 1970s, it features an upholstered seat cushion and two tubular components that form a continuous line of legs, armrests and backrests. The structure can be dismantled and the materials are recyclable. Urquiola imagined the piece as a space of conviviality and leisure, the beating heart of the home. "It adapts to our changing needs: a daybed, a soft desk, a place for conversation and connection," she says. "It supports togetherness, flexibility and shared time. Sometimes I lie across it with a book; sometimes I sit cross-legged on it with my laptop and a green tea. It doesn't ask you to sit in just one way – it invites."

This empathetic approach is what guides Urquiola through all of her projects, finding new ways to make unique, durable pieces using materials that not only provide comfort but reconnect us to the environment. "For me, it's about finding a new language for the beauty of regeneration, constantly flipping the relationship between what we think of as ugly and what we consider beautiful," she says. "It's crucial to factor in the end of a product's life from the very beginning: how it can be disassembled, how its components might be reused and what its overall footprint will be."

Sofa designer
Patricia Urquiola

Manufacturer
Cassina

Year designed
2025

About the sofa
As art director at Cassina, Urquiola plays a significant role in guiding its creative output. The chunky silhouette and curved form of this sofa were inspired by the joyful styles of 1970s design. Made to be easily disassembled, the materials used for the Dudet Bold have been chosen to be recycled after use. This piece is a testament to Urquiola's dedication to sustainable design and Cassina's signature craftsmanship.

About the owner
Patricia Urquiola is a Spanish industrial designer and architect known for her innovative, poetic approach. She opened her studio in Milan in 2001 and her work spans furniture, interiors and architecture, blending craftsmanship with cutting-edge technology. A number of her works have been acquired by significant institutions including New York's Museum of Modern Art, the Musée des Arts Décoratifs in Paris and the Victoria and Albert Museum in London.

09.
John Wardle
On the Gentry sofa

Melbourne, Australia

For John Wardle, many sofas have come and gone. One, however, has had staying power: Moroso's Gentry. This cherished piece, with its distinct legs and deep seats, is an irreplaceable family fixture, a testament to its ability to blend comfort with functionality.

Sofa designer
Patricia Urquiola

Manufacturer
Moroso

Year designed
2011

About the sofa
The Gentry sofa, designed by Spanish designer Patricia Urquiola, is a modern reimagining of classic luxury. Urquiola's design has a refined, minimalist silhouette, which she characterises as "basic simplicity". An elegant addition to the predominantly rectilinear sofa is a curve to the outer back and side arms, creating a gently scalloped profile when seen from above. In 2018 the Gentry Extra Light was launched, a compact design making the Gentry an option for a larger range of spaces.

About the owner
Melbourne-based John Wardle is an architect's architect known for his meticulous attention to detail and a profound connection to place. Over the course of more than 30 years, he has built a practice that specialises in numerous building types, from small dwellings to university buildings, museums, public spaces, high-density housing and large commercial offices. Wardle has garnered numerous accolades, including the prestigious Australian Institute of Architects Gold Medal in 2020, celebrating a career of impactful and finely-crafted buildings.

John Wardle has had encounters with many sofas. His first major postgraduate purchase was a custom-made sofa that he still cherishes – and lounges on – regularly. Early in the esteemed Melbourne-based architect's career, Wardle also designed a couch pro bono for his local hairdresser. "They paid me in haircuts for over a decade," says Wardle. Once, while helping to move a sofa, wayward octopus straps struck Wardle in the eye, landing him in hospital for a week and nearly blinding him.

But the architect's eyes were once even more pained by a client's decision to use a lurid, yellow, banana-shaped couch in an interior. So much so that he and the client's wife conspired to have it removed and replaced with more aesthetically consonant furniture. "But he sprung us and got home from his business trip early," says Wardle. "His wife and I got into a lot of trouble." When Wardle and his wife, Susan, started a family, another sofa snafu awaited them – a white sofa, purchased on sale, couldn't withstand a young family. "We sold it after six months to an architect who didn't have children."

But Wardle's couch fortunes changed when he acquired a brown Gentry sofa by Italian furniture firm Moroso. "As many sofas as we've had over the course of a long marriage – and we've had so many – I always wanted a big brown-leather sofa," says Wardle of the Italian-made couch. "This is the one."

Wardle is a long-time admirer of its renowned designer, Spanish-born and Italy-based Patricia Urquiola (see page 36). That appreciation only grew following visits to each other's studios in Melbourne and Milan, respectively. Another layer that deepens Wardle's connection with the Gentry is his link to Patrizia Moroso, art director for Moroso. The pair were introduced many years ago and Moroso even stayed at Wardle's cottage on Bruny Island in Tasmania when she visited Australia.

Moroso and Urquiola's Australian travels impacted this Gentry sofa's design too. Wardle's couch is a limited release, with russet-red steel legs. "Patricia brought out this limited edition with these beautiful legs inspired by the colours that she saw in Australia's beautiful red centre."

For Wardle, the sofa plays a fundamental – if underappreciated – role in a home. "A good sofa allows for every aspect of human engagement, from leaning forward in deep conversation to slumping back and reading a book," he says. "They might be less singularly demanding to design than a dining chair but

"Whenever I'm in the early schematic design for a home, the first thing I sketch is the couch"

whenever I'm in the early schematic design for a home, the first thing I sketch is the couch. It's a central aspect of sociability in the house." The Gentry, with its low back and deep seat, can play every role that Wardle casts it in.

The Wardles recently sold their long-time family home, Kew Residence. And despite the fact that they lived in the home far longer than the Gentry was in place there, the sofa has become irreplaceable. "We're not sure where we're going next and our other sofa is being sacrificed to our changing lifestyle," says Wardle. "But the Gentry had to be the one to come with us." Before moving out, three generations of Wardles gathered for one last family photo. They took it in their favourite part of the house, all together on the Gentry sofa.

10.
Sabine Marcelis
& Paul Cournet
On the Lisse sofa

Rotterdam,
Netherlands

Can a sofa bring a workplace
together? Sabine Marcelis's Lisse
does, anchoring her Rotterdam
studio's liveliness with its gentle
curves. It transforms from a
team brainstorming hub into an
intimate dining spot, emphasising
the potential of furniture to grow
and adapt to the needs of users.

Sofa designer
Sabine Marcelis

Manufacturer
La Cividina

Year designed
2025

About the sofa
It's often said that the simplest ideas are the hardest to execute well. A case in point is the Lisse sofa, which relies on the know-how of Italian manufacturer La Cividina to deliver its minimal silhouette. Based in the northeast of Italy, the company was founded in 1976 and has since pioneered an artisanal approach to manufacturing, combining manual skills with state-of-the-art production methods. With the use of a beech frame and meticulous upholstering methods, the result is a purity of form that appears deceptively effortless.

About the owners
Sabine Marcelis is celebrated for her use of translucent materials (think resin, acrylic and glass) rendered in soft, rounded shapes. A leading figure in the contemporary design landscape, the Rotterdam-based creative has had pieces acquired by The Museum of Modern Art in New York and the Vitra Design Museum in Germany. Working at the intersection of light, form and colour, she has collaborated with the likes of Swedish design giant Ikea and Italian luxury fashion house Fendi. Marcelis has also collaborated with her partner, Paul Cournet (*pictured, previous page*), the founder of multi-disciplinary studio Cloud, on numerous projects.

As a designer, Sabine Marcelis has played a hand in defining the look and feel of the early 21st century. The Dutch creative's vision has graced the catalogues of manufacturers including Acerbis and Vitra, as well as a wildly popular range of homeware for Ikea. Her prolific body of work, while mostly focused on product and artistic installations, also includes the Lisse (French for "smooth"), a sofa produced by Italian manufacturer La Cividina and launched in 2025.

With a sculptural, sinuous profile, the five-seater sits in Marcelis's studio in Rotterdam, where it acts as a site for team gatherings,

"Sofas are like bodies that can be dressed in different clothes. It can easily be reupholstered when the fabric gets tired"

brainstorming sessions, lunches and meetings with regular collaborators – including her partner, French architect Paul Cournet. "Sofas are objects to be lived with and on," says Marcelis. "It will get a stain at some point and then you just get a professional cleaning job. I don't want to be pedantic – especially because I don't know where else I'd like to eat lunch." It's a brave approach to living with design, considering Marcelis's choice of a beige colourway for the upholstery of this particular piece.

According to Marcelis, the neutral hue and simplicity of the design brings a touch of tranquility to her workspace. "The sofa is a calming constant within the turmoil of the ever-changing artworks around it," she says. "I also wanted to push this idea of softness. It's quite different for me to design something that has a soft materiality because I'm always working with hard materials such as resin, glass and natural stone."

The result is a sofa with a pleasingly round, almost futuristic quality that wouldn't look out of place on the set of Stanley Kubrick's 1968 film *2001: A Space Odyssey*. It is built using a sturdy beech-and-fir skeleton that is then padded and upholstered in a recycled polyester fabric by Dutch brand Febrik. Stretched over the body of the sofa, the result is a crease-free look that is sewn into position along two discreet seams. "Sofas are like bodies that can be dressed in different clothes," she adds. "It can easily be reupholstered when the fabric gets tired. It changes the whole vibe of a sofa."

When it came to considering the proportions of the piece, Marcelis says that the height of the backrest was key to ensuring Lisse doesn't just look good but is comfortable as well. "It's also very functional because it has all these additional elements that can be added," she says, referring to the extra ottomans and seats that can be brought in, while echoing the curved shape of the main body of the sofa. "When people visit we can pull up more seating. It's adaptable but in an easy way: you just pull pieces over rather than reconfiguring it entirely. I'm always looking for flexibility in my designs – I wanted to create something that grows with you as a person, a family or a studio."

II.
Joris Poggioli
On the Patrick sofa

Paris, France

The story behind the name of Joris Poggioli's sofa is a personal one. "Patrick is a member of the team, who helps us develop everything we draw – including this sofa," says the French-Italian designer, who runs Paris-based studio and brand Youth Éditions. "Once we had it developed, after almost 20 prototypes, I thought the least he deserved was having the sofa named after him."

The resulting modular sofa is a testament to Poggioli's – and clearly Patrick's – bold and sculptural design language. Produced for his own furniture line, the striking piece is defined by distinctive geometric blocks upholstered in premium leather. The modules can then be assembled to form an endless number of configurations, making it an ideal perch for spaces ranging from compact Parisian apartments to grand chateaux. But, regardless of the room or environment the sofa is placed in, it retains an inviting presence, marrying luxurious comfort with strong architectural form – a language that shouldn't be a surprise for those who know Poggioli.

After studying architecture in Paris while simultaneously sculpting in his uncle's art studio, a young Poggioli practised as an architect for seven years before venturing out as a designer in his own right in 2017. As such, his inspiration ranges from French design icons such as Pierre Paulin to Italian mid-century furniture and architecture maestro Joe Colombo, with Poggioli prioritising sculptural form over function. His ideal sofa, then, is not only a pile of pillows to sink into but an expression of taste. "Some people are obsessed with comfort," he says. "My vision is to please the eyes first, because comfort for the eyes is comfort for the brain."

Indeed, the Patrick is the perfect embodiment of this idea, standing as a focal point in Poggioli's living room with the statement piece inviting both interaction and admiration – and still serving its owner's everyday life. "I love hosting guests," says Poggioli. "I enjoy lying down. I adore watching cinema. I love accommodating friends who stay over. Patrick gives me these options."

Sofa designer
Joris Poggioli

Manufacturer
Youth Éditions

Year designed
2024

About the sofa
Joris Poggioli's Patrick sofa is a testament to bold, sculptural design. It is defined by its distinctive modular blocks, which can be assembled in different configurations. Marrying a strong architectural form with luxurious comfort, the sofa is meticulously crafted with a robust internal frame and premium leather upholstery. The resulting piece adds a contemporary edge to classic French grandeur, offering deep, tactile comfort.

About the owner
Joris Poggioli is an architect and designer who creates furniture blending his dual heritages: French elegance meets Italian eccentricity. After studying architecture, he established his Youth Éditions practice in 2017. Its work prioritises emotion, disrupting conventional furniture through the translation of shape and materiality. The results are pieces that can transform spaces with a commanding presence, blurring art and design, and bringing a touch of playfulness to any interior.

12.
Betty Ng
*On the
Marenco sofa*

Hong Kong,
China

Betty Ng spent years treating sofas as afterthoughts – makeshift seating for her nomadic lifestyle. Everything changed when she decided to settle on an apartment and her first "serious" sofa: a pillow-like Arflex piece that is a symbol of permanence and confidence.

Sofa designer
Mario Marenco

Manufacturer
Arflex

Year designed
1970

About the sofa
Mario Marenco created this sofa for Italian manufacturer Arflex in 1970, which is now celebrated for its unique construction. Its substantial cushions – comprising individual elements for the back, seat and arms – are engineered with different densities for support and softness. These sections are then inserted into a hidden tubular metal frame, providing the sofa with essential rigidity. It's a construction that allows for modularity, while ensuring that the Marenco maintains its invitingly plump profile.

About the owner
Hong Kong-based architect Betty Ng established her studio, Collective, in 2015 after stints at OMA and Herzog & de Meuron. The practice takes a research and concept-driven approach, eschewing repetitive styles to create unique works across architecture, interiors and exhibition design. Notable projects include the Christie's Asia-Pacific headquarters and the podium for 83 King Lam Street in Hong Kong, which transformed an industrial site into a pixelated landscape of green public terraces with reconfigurable auditorium spaces underneath.

For years, architect Betty Ng never gave much thought to the sofa, either as a design object or as a piece of proper furniture. "I moved around a lot and I lived in fairly compact spaces," says the founder and director of Hong Kong-based architecture firm Collective. "So, I usually had something makeshift for me to sit or lie on. It was never something that held meaning." That changed when she moved into an apartment in Hong Kong, where she decided to stay for the long haul. Here, for the first time, Ng invested in what she calls a "serious" sofa: a two-seater by Arflex, designed in 1970 by Italian

"In a way, the sofa became a symbol of being able to settle down and it allowed me to feel like I'm home. It gave me softness and comfort"

architect Mario Marenco. "It fits the space perfectly. In a way, it became a symbol of being able to settle down and it allowed me to feel like I'm home," says Ng. "It gave me softness and comfort."

Today, the sofa serves as more than just a seat. It's where the architect unwinds at the end of the day, watches Netflix shows, eats dinner and takes the occasional nap. The sofa anchors a warm living space that is lush with greenery. Flanking it is a monstera, three large fiddle-leaf figs and a two-metre-high polka-dot begonia; all signs of a home that's been truly made her own. Behind the

sofa hangs a triptych painting by her former boss Rem Koolhaas that she purchased at an auction, while a nearby bookshelf holds mementos from her travels. The room feels comfortable and personal, a fitting canvas for a sofa that looks like six fluffy, oversized pillows assembled together.

Upholstered in off-white, wool Kvadrat fabric – a material Ng uses in her own designs – the sofa at first glance looks deceptively soft. "Pillows are usually white and I wanted to honour the concept," she says. "But because the sofa looks so much like a pillow, you think it's going to be fluffy. It's not, but no one expects to sit on two giant pillows and feel supported. It really holds you." Comfort and firmness, says Ng, were essential and this piece delivers on both fronts.

The Marenco's modular, seamless construction also won Ng over, which she likens to a very sophisticated Ikea system that's easy to disassemble, clean and reassemble. "It's not just so-called high-end design, but it's incredibly smart and intuitive too. Taking it apart and putting it back together feels like a well-choreographed dance." Ng and her partner each claim a "pillow" when they sit, facing the wall onto which their short-range projector casts films and TV programmes.

The sofa has made such an impression that Ng is now considering adding a Marenco armchair to the mix. "The concept is extremely clear. It's slightly whimsical and I feel it's the type of design that reflects how we design as a studio: clear, intentional and playful," she says. "The simplicity speaks to me and anything that's designed with purpose and executed with purity really resonates with me."

13.
Farshid Moussavi
On the Osaka sofa

London, UK

Iranian-born, London-based architect Farshid Moussavi selected a five-metre-long sofa to emphasise her living room's scale. While it primarily serves as a place for laid-back socialising, its presence provides a visual and physical focal point for the entire household.

Sofa designer
Pierre Paulin

Manufacturer
La Cividina

Year designed
1967

About the sofa
This sofa by French designer Pierre Paulin for Italian manufacturer La Cividina embodies sophisticated versatility. Defined by its clean, geometric lines and balanced proportions, its comfort is meticulously engineered thanks to a multi-density foam seat, ensuring lasting support beneath its tailored upholstery. Composed of modular elements, the Osaka allows for countless configurations, from expansive linear arrangements to corner compositions or standalone pieces – making it suited for both public spaces and private residences.

About the owner
Farshid Moussavi was born in Iran and educated at Harvard University, London's Bartlett School of Architecture and Dundee University. She established Farshid Moussavi Architecture in 2011, championing an ethos of "performative architecture" that embraces complexity and rejects fixed styles. Her global portfolio of projects includes the Yokohama International Ferry Terminal, an undulating public landscape; the Museum of Contemporary Art Cleveland, with its faceted steel skin; and the Edificio Bambú social housing project in Madrid.

"My living room is tall and long so I can choose furniture that wouldn't work in a smaller place," says Farshid Moussavi. This space in her London home naturally calls for a sofa that can match it – and this impressively proportioned version of the Osaka sofa does just that. "I'm an architect, so I choose my furniture according to the dimensions of the space I have and the designers I admire," says Moussavi. The Iranian-born British architect had always had French designer Pierre Paulin's creations in mind when she was furnishing her flat. Paulin's work is defined by organic forms, technological

"I'm an architect, so I choose my furniture according to the dimensions of the space I have and the designers I admire"

innovation and a deep concern for human comfort and experience – and his resulting Osaka model sofa, which ticks these boxes, was an obvious choice for Moussavi.

Designed for Italian furniture firm La Cividina, Moussavi's version of Paulin's customisable sofa is black and a sizeable five metres in length. "Metal brackets on the base mean that you can shape and curve it to suit your needs," says Moussavi. "I was interested in the idea that I could change the look of the piece over time." The architect believes that any good sofa requires some level of customisation to suit the space that it's in,

whether it's in terms of the fabric chosen or the number of modules that it is composed of. "This sofa actually looks better when it's longer," says Moussavi. "I was interested in the fact that I could celebrate the length of the space rather than seeing it as a hindrance." She adds that her choice of a monochrome colour palette has also provided the backdrop for a level of colourful personalisation. One of her daughter's drawings of a green tortoise has been made into a cushion to give the perch its own identity.

Moussavi spends most of her working day sitting down, so her spare time when she is alone is spent up and about, away from the sofa. "It means that I associate my Osaka with sitting down with someone else rather than relaxing alone. When I'm off duty, I'm moving around." The Osaka model therefore holds fond memories of warm gatherings with family and friends. "My flat holds nostalgic memories of my daughter growing up," says Moussavi. "The sofa was put to good use when she'd have birthday parties here. It could easily hold all of her friends."

While its role in providing a social space in the home is important, Moussavi says that ultimately comfort and timelessness are key. "It's very important that the back isn't too far away from the edge of the seat, so your feet aren't floating and your spine is straight. The foam should be firm and the fabric should be tactile and robust so it lasts and stays cleaner for longer," says Moussavi, adding that the Osaka succeeds brilliantly on all these fronts and more. "It's a simple, sculptural piece that is completely timeless. But it's also very recognisable and gives a sense of place to my living room."

14.
Eran Chen
*On the
Extrasoft sofa*

New York, USA

Eran Chen's 12-seater Extrasoft commands views of two aspects of his home – one side for wine and celebration, the other for movie nights with a strict no-food rule. It's a bold piece of furniture, cleverly positioned to accommodate a range of activities, reflecting Chen's ethos.

Sofa designer
Piero Lissoni

Manufacturer
Living Divani

Year designed
2008

About the sofa
The Extrasoft is a modular seating system that features low, upholstered geometric blocks, allowing for various configurations, including, notably, a central spine with seating facing in opposite directions and occupants sitting back to back. Its construction emphasises comfort, incorporating a multi-density polyurethane foam core on a double-panelled poplar frame, enveloped by quilted goose-down padding. The resulting sofa embodies Piero Lissoni's minimalist aesthetic, offering adaptability, a plush, yielding comfort and infinite permutations.

About the owner
Eran Chen founded his architecture, interior-design and landscape-design practice ODA in New York in 2007. His approach to practice prioritises the integration of natural light, green space and amenities into structures, challenging traditional urban typologies. Notable works include 420 Kent, a striking Brooklyn apartment building with a multi-dimensional façade to maximise views and outdoor spaces for residents, and the adaptive reuse of Detroit's historic Book Tower, which he transformed into a vibrant mixed-use hub with shared, grand public spaces.

"It anchors the living room and each one of us has a different corner that we like," says Eran Chen. The New York-based architect is referring to the Extrasoft modular sofa that belongs to his family of five. Designed by Milan-based Piero Lissoni for Italian firm Living Divani, it comfortably seats up to eight people and can be moved around, making it a versatile seating option for his family.

"As a family, we wanted something that's much more free-form and flexible in terms of its experience," says Chen. Enter the Extrasoft, whose size and shape allows for a variety of configurations, encouraging people to come together – an appropriate outcome, given that the Chen family made a group decision to purchase the sofa and finish it in a vintage red colour. "Red is not a traditional or safe colour for a sofa," adds Chen of the collaborative colour choice. "But we all decided that it was the bright spot that energised and centred the entire palette of the room."

Adding to the communal feeling imbued in the sofa is the fact that it is also double-sided and faces two sides of the Chen family home: the kitchen and dining area in one direction and the projector in the main living-room in the other. "Very strict rules apply to the different sides," says Chen. On the living room side, where the family watches movies, no drinks and food are allowed. But on the other side, they've been known to open a bottle of wine. "We celebrate on the sofa all the time," he says. When his daughter was waiting for her acceptance email into her chosen university, the entire family sat on the couch all hunched over a laptop awaiting the news. When they learned that she was accepted they jumped up on top of it and started dancing. "All five of us," says Chen, recalling the occasion with a laugh. "Even the dog."

Given the sofa's size, there are many nooks its users can occupy but Chen has a favourite seat overlooking the kitchen and windows. "That's my spot," he says, adding that when he gets in from work he likes to settle into the sofa and have a conversation with his wife. "It gives me a sense of connection to my home." The couch is used for everything: movies, board games, karaoke and even a bed for his kids' friends. "Sometimes I wake up in the morning and there are several people on the sofa," he says.

The fact that the Extrasoft is so adaptable makes sense considering Chen loves the idea of multifunctionality and multi-experiences – traits that are woven into his work. "How can a sofa accommodate our bodies in different ways?" he asks. "That is the most interesting part in designing furniture – beyond the details, textures and proportions."

For Chen, one of the main elements of a good sofa is comfort. "I don't believe in things that look good but don't feel good," he says, adding that couches should be casual enough that people can sit down without worrying that they might damage or stain it. "At the end of the day, the sofa is the main place of gathering where we want to feel togetherness and comfort. There are certain sofas that look good but make you feel anxious and nervous. You want something you can sink into and feel very casual and comfortable on."

"I haven't seen many successful sofas that are petite. For me, the meaning of a sofa comes with size and the ability for many people to enjoy it"

15.
Yinka Ilori
On a custom-upcycled sofa

London, UK

"Honestly, we bought them on Ebay," says designer Yinka Ilori, surveying the pair of unbranded – and now upcycled – two-seater sofas that face each other at the back of his studio in London. For those familiar with the London native's work, it shouldn't come as a surprise that his sofa of choice is upcycled. "I am fascinated by the power of reloving and reimagining objects that have stories that exist already," says Ilori, of the pair of sofas that were originally made for a pop-up shop that he hosted at east London's Hoxton Hotel in 2024. "I like the way that you can transform them."

In an area of industrial estates, ghost kitchens and factories, his workplace – in which the sofas feature prominently – is a lone island of colour and pattern. The unit is filled with the work that he has produced since his career began in 2009, practising at every scale from homeware to bridges. Pointing to the thick folds of new skirting around the upcycled sofa's bases, he says, "These little details were all the existing ones. We kept them exactly the same as they were originally in terms of silhouette, the pleats of the fabric and the curve of the armrests."

The sofas' transformation involved recovering them in a tightly woven woollen fabric that he had made in the US. From a distance, the fabric has a hypnotic, pop-art quality. Up close, it resolves into a repeating pattern of red and orange feathers set against a deep purple. "It's about dream catchers," says Ilori

of the pattern, which he designed. "Within my world of design and art, dreams and dreaming are things that I really hold close to my heart."

Indeed, with their rounded edges, soft cushions and tactile fabric, Ilori's upgrade lures the revamped two-seater into that dreamy state perfectly. "It's the sort of sofa that you sink into – you want to have a sleep or a nap on it. It's a sofa that I hope inspires affirmation and positivity."

Sofa designer
Yinka Ilori

Manufacturer
Momentum Textiles
& Wallcovering (fabric)

Year designed
2024

About the sofa
Yinka Ilori has made frequent use of upcycled furniture during his career. These pieces have deep cushions, curved bulbous arms and floor-length skirting. Reupholstered in a fabric designed by Ilori and specially made by Momentum Textiles & Wallcovering in Irvine, California, the tightly woven textile is titled

Dream Catchers
after the repeating
feather pattern.

About the owner
British-Nigerian multi-disciplinary artist and designer Yinka Ilori is known for his vibrant creations that draw inspiration from his heritage. His work spans interior and furniture design, public installations, architectural projects and graphic design. The outcome often evokes a sense of optimism, with key projects such as the Flamboyance of Flamingos, a wildlife-inspired playground on the Becontree Estate, London (2022).

16.
Steven Holl &
Dimitra Tsachrelia
On the Club sofa

Rhinebeck,
New York State,
USA

Needing to refresh their
vintage Jean-Michel Frank
sofa, architects Steven Holl
and Dimitra Tsachrelia gave
creative control to their nine-
year-old daughter. The result
is a demonstration that design
can be enhanced by inviting
unexpected inputs.

Sofa designer
Jean-Michel Frank

Manufacturer
Ecart International

Year designed
1930

About the sofa
Designed in the 1930s by French interior designer Jean-Michel Frank, this sofa was used in Frank's own interiors. Composed of a series of strict, rectilinear volumes, it features low, squared armrests that align perfectly with the backrest to form a continuous horizontal plane, while the deep seat appears almost monolithic in its presence. Produced in France by Paris-based Ecart International, it is built by hand and features a solid wood frame with oak feet.

About the owner
Architect, theorist, teacher and watercolourist Steven Holl established his namesake practice in 1977, which he runs with his wife, Dimitra Tsachrelia. The duo now have offices in New York, Hudson Valley and Beijing, working on projects across the globe with portfolio highlights including the Kiasma Museum of Contemporary Art in Helsinki, Hunters Point Library in Queens, the Chapel of St Ignatius in Seattle and the Daeyang Gallery and House in South Korea.

It takes a lot for two world-class architects to surrender creative control – especially over the furniture in their own living room. But that's exactly what Steven Holl and his wife, Dimitra Tsachrelia, did when it was time to reupholster their decades-old Jean-Michel Frank Club sofa in their home in Rhinebeck, New York State. The minimalist three-seater, originally in Bauhaus-grey, had been a reliable centrepiece of their 1952 stone-and-wood cottage. Worn by years of family life – dogs, dinners, Dr Seuss readings and Swedish pancake breakfasts – it was due for a refresh. But rather than opt for a tasteful

"The more I looked at her drawing of the sofa, the more it made sense. It had joy. It had intent"

neutral or the black that Holl had in mind, they handed the reins to someone else: their nine-year-old daughter, Io.

"I went to pick up a black sample and came back with a rainbow of swatches," says Tsachrelia, who is principal-in-charge at her husband's namesake practice, Steven Holl Architects. "I thought, let's just engage the kids and play." What followed was an impressive sketch from Io and a family debate over her vision: a bold composition of green seat cushions, orange backs and pink sides. "At first, I recoiled a bit," says Holl. "The architect in me wanted restraint and something

neutral, subdued. But the more I looked at her drawing, the more it made sense. It had joy. It had intent." In short, Io's vision for the sofa renewal won over her parents, prompting the family to enlist a Hudson Valley upholsterer to bring her design to life, crafting new covers in the bright palette.

The result: not only a transformed sofa but an evolved family dynamic. "Imagine being nine, sketching your idea and then seeing it come to life," says Holl, with a mix of reflection and delight. "Sometimes things need to go to the next generation." Indeed, the transformed sofa is more than just furniture – it's now a generational artifact, a family anchor that both children and parents can lay claim to. It sits at the heart of the Holls' U-shaped home, facing the fireplace, hosting everything from family games and dancing shows to a napping Silky, the family labrador. "We don't have any rules in our house," says Holl. "It's complete chaos."

Indeed, while the home and the family's apartment in New York City contain design treasures – Frank Lloyd Wright chairs, a Le Corbusier chaise, even a rare Robert Mallet-Stevens prototype – none of it is preserved behind velvet ropes. "Living with Steven, I've learned that furniture isn't treated as a design object," says Tsachrelia. "It's really lived in." Even the prized pieces bear the signs of daily life: slight chew marks from pets, stains from syrup, footprints from being used as a launchpad for backflips.

The sofa, like much of Holl's work, resists the idea of design as frozen perfection. His own early interiors were never meant for mass production. They were about the place, the geometry, the people. This reimagined family sofa, inspired not by theory or current tastes but by childhood creativity, carries that spirit forward.

17.
Nada Debs
On the Zen sofa

Dubai, UAE

Nada Debs designed the Zen
sofa to encourage connection
and conversation. Appropriately,
the work also seamlessly fuses
Middle Eastern craft with
Japanese minimalism. The
outcome is a sofa that's both a
personal sanctuary and a perfect
setting for lively gatherings.

Sofa designer
Nada Debs

Manufacturer
Studio Nada Debs

Year designed
2021

About the sofa
The Zen sofa is a perfect fusion of contemporary style and traditional craftsmanship. The design is inspired by Debs's commitment to creating furniture that blends influences from both East and West, reflecting her Lebanese heritage, her childhood spent in Japan and her international design sensibilities. The sofa features clean, minimalistic lines with a hand-carved timber base, while it is upholstered in a simple, unadorned fabric.

About the owner
Lebanese designer Nada Debs is celebrated for her finely-crafted furniture and large-scale interior-design projects. Both draw on her international background: raised in Japan, Debs studied at the Rhode Island School of Design in the US before working in the UK and then establishing a globally renowned design studio in Beirut. Now splitting her time between the Lebanese capital and Dubai, she is a champion of regional craftsmanship in the Middle East.

When Nada Debs was planning the layout of her Dubai home's living room, she chose not one but two of her own Zen sofas. Shaped like a quarter circle, the Lebanese designer positioned them to face each other. "When people sit on them both, we create one circle and can easily face one another," says Debs. "Sitting then becomes a very communal experience. It's something that is much nicer when you're with other people and quite different to being on a straight sofa, which makes you look out or away from the space. Here, you're always directed back into the middle."

The sofa is part of Debs' namesake brand's Now & Zen collection, which is inspired by contemporary Japan. The sofa design is personal. It connects her to a childhood spent growing up in Kobe, Japan, after her family relocated there from Lebanon in the early 20th century. "It was my great uncle who first came to Japan in 1917 as a merchant travelling down the Silk Road, trading in textiles," she says. "I've always felt like I'm a global citizen, not quite belonging in either Lebanon or Japan. So, my work is about combining the influence of Middle Eastern craft with Japan's minimalist design."

That comes through in the linen fabric that covers the sofa – reminiscent, to Debs, of Japanese *washi* paper – while the low base of the Zen sofa gives a futon-like feel to the piece; an extended, non-cushioned section of timber creates an additional table setting. "Its beauty also lies in the intricate carvings on the edge of the wood, which give the sofa a lot of texture."

Following the 2020 Beirut explosion that devastated large parts of the city, Debs moved to Dubai. But her links to the Lebanese capital – and Japan – have not been lost in the relocation process. "Fusing together Japan and Lebanon in this sofa lets me connect the two cultures that I grew up with. It's a hybrid that helps me feel at home wherever I am." Though Debs no longer lives in Japan, her mother and brother still do and she travels back there every year. "Whenever I'm designing, all the Japanese influences that surrounded me in my childhood just surface," she says. "It's in my subconscious."

But as much as the sofa is a symbolic way for Debs to reconcile the various cultures that have made up her life and connect her with a family that is spread across countries and continents, it is a practical piece of furniture. "When I was designing it, it was vital to me that it was comfortable," says Debs. "I chose the right cushion density, so it wasn't

"Fusing together Japan and Lebanon in this sofa lets me connect the two cultures I grew up with"

too rigid or too loose. The angle of the backrest is also perfect for leaning back, so I often meditate here." And despite its name, Debs's pair of Zen sofas are also perfect for hosting parties and gatherings. "When people swing by for a quick visit and say they'll only be able to stay for half an hour, they'll end up lingering for two, just sitting in the same position," says Debs. "The sofas bring people together. To me, it's proof that they're comfortable enough."

18.
Jay Osgerby
On the Elan sofa

London, UK

Jay Osgerby's relationship with a pair of Jasper Morrison sofas began as a leap of design faith as a newlywed. They have become lifelong companions and seen countless family landmarks, from house moves to childbirth – a reminder of the relationships that good design can facilitate.

Sofa designer
Jasper Morrison

Manufacturer
Cappellini

Year designed
1999

About the sofa
Jasper Morrison's Elan sofa, designed for Italian manufacturer Cappellini, epitomises the British creative's "super normal" design philosophy, pioneered by Morrison (*see page 90*) with Naoto Fukasawa (*page 74*) – an approach that eschews novelty for simple practicality. Its understated yet refined presence belies a robust construction, featuring a plywood frame and polyurethane foam with feather-stuffed cushions for comfort. Characterised by clean lines and generous proportions, the Elan is the perfect fit for any space looking to accommodate a robust home-life – an enduring piece that prioritises quiet utility and lasting elegance over fleeting trends.

About the owner
Jay Osgerby met his long-time design and business partner Edward Barber at London's Royal College of Art in the 1990s. Over the ensuing decades, they founded their namesake studio – Barber Osgerby – as well as design firms Universal Design Studio and Map Project Office. Their diverse portfolio of work spans industrial design, furniture and public commissions, with clients including Vitra, Knoll, B&B Italia, Flos and Hermès. Stand-out projects include the London 2012 Olympic Torch and designs for the UK's Royal Mint.

London-based architect and industrial designer Jay Osgerby knows more than a thing or two about design. With Barber Osgerby, the studio he co-founded with Edward Barber in 1996, he has worked on furniture, lighting and product design – as well as art and architecture – for clients including Knoll, B&B Italia and Vitra. As such, he's designed a number of sofas. "A sofa is an expression of design meets manufacturing prowess, meets structural engineering, meets the human body," says Osgerby, before adding that the most important relationship he has with one is not with one of his own designs. Rather, it's with a matching pair of Elan sofas by Jasper Morrison (*see page 90*) that he has owned for almost a quarter of a century.

In 1999, Osgerby and his partner, Helen, bought their first home together – a small garden flat in south London. At the time they had no furniture and the two Elans were the biggest financial commitment they had ever made, other than the home itself. "Those sofas are a real testimony to Jasper's vision and his approach to design," says Osgerby. "One of the things I've always loved about his work – and it's a quality I aspire to myself – is his ability to create pieces of furniture that become friends you want to live with

"People often talk about visual comfort, but it's a conceit because something can be visually comfortable and then really let you down when you sit on it"

your whole life – rather than protagonists who always want to take centre stage."

The Elans have turned out to be an integral part of the Osgerby family's life. Their three children were all born after the arrival of the sofas, which have at various times doubled as feeding stations and even a delivery table. "My son Felix was born on the Elan," says Osgerby, laughing. "Thinking about it now – that's just mad." The latest addition to the family, a dog called Enzo, has taken up a permanent surveillance position on one of the sofas. From here, sitting on a specially made loose cover, he monitors all of the action in the kitchen – proof that the sofas have become integral parts of the family's life. "Not for a second have I thought about swapping them," says Osgerby. "They've moved house with us three times and all I've ever done is have them reupholstered every five or six years."

Despite this attachment, it doesn't mean Osgerby is closed off to the idea of other sofas in other homes. "We're converting a barn into a weekend home," says Osgerby. "When that's done, I'll be installing a Mariposa." One of Osgerby's own designs in collaboration with Edward Barber, the Mariposa for Swiss firm Vitra expresses the duo's fascination with movement. The arms are the same height as the back in their fully upright position but can be adjusted into reclined planes that enable sitters to lounge and stretch out, with multiple options for propped elbows and supported heads. "I have to say that a sofa is the hardest thing to design," says Osgerby of the process to create the Mariposa, which adds to his appreciation for Morrison's Elan. "Unlike a chair, you're not making something for a person to sit on in one position. With a sofa, you have to allow for an unlimited range of ergonomic variations. It almost puts you off doing it, if I'm honest!"

19.
Naoto Fukasawa
On the Hiroshima sofa

Tokyo, Japan

"I wanted to create an atelier," says Naoto Fukasawa. "This is an office and also a home and all of the objects are designed and used by me." The Japanese designer's studio-cum-residence in Tokyo's Setagaya neighbourhood is a testing ground for his products. The L-shaped structure has tall windows overlooking a tranquil garden, with a workspace and workshop for his team on the ground and basement floors. Above, the first floor serves as Fukasawa's private residence, connected by a black spiral staircase. And it's at the top of these stairs that his three-seater Hiroshima sofa, which he designed for Japanese brand Maruni, sits.

The decision to place it here speaks to Fukasawa's atelier project, where he has designed every detail of the space, from the lighting and furniture to the tableware. The sofa, says the designer, was always going to go in this location, even if it had to be lifted through a top-floor window. "People often design houses without a thought for the sofa that they are going to choose," says Fukasawa of the decision to use the Hiroshima despite the challenges of getting it inside. "They focus on the building budget first and then, after, they think, 'Oh, we need to choose furniture,' and end up with something less than ideal." Such an approach, says Fukasawa, should be turned on its head to deliver the best interior environments – and his upstairs living room and Hiroshima sofa combination is a case in point. Here, in a space bathed in natural light, the designer can be found drawing, reading and holding meetings. "You don't sit face to face but next to each other," says Fukasawa. "You can be more conversational, easy and natural."

The proportions of the sofa are perfect for the space, something that was taken into consideration when designing it. "It is way smaller than a European sofa, which usually has a huge depth – but that's not really sellable in the Japanese market as our homes are smaller," says Fukasawa. "I modified the sofa so that it will fit in Japan and have the right balance. It's a simple icon."

Sofa designer
Naoto Fukasawa

Manufacturer
Maruni

Year designed
2009

About the sofa
The Hiroshima sofa collection, designed by Naoto Fukasawa for Japanese brand Maruni, is characterised by gentle, welcoming curves and seamless craftsmanship that features a solid wood frame, complemented by plush upholstery. A modular system, it offers components including L-shaped seating, integrated armrests and versatile pouffes, enabling bespoke configurations.

About the owner
Naoto Fukasawa is one of the leading lights in contemporary design. The Japanese creative graduated from Tama Art University in Tokyo and honed his craft at world-renowned San Franciscan firm ID Two, before establishing his own namesake practice in Tokyo in 2003. Since then he has developed his "super normal" design philosophy for clients including Muji, Apple and Maruni, with Fukasawa's work consistently elevating the everyday.

20.
Yuichi Kodai &
Claudia Maggi
On the Sumo sofa

Zürich,
Switzerland

Architects Yuichi Kodai and
Claudia Maggi found their ideal
sofa in Living Divani's sleek
Sumo. It's a low-slung, elegant
design, offering those perching
on it a unique perspective of
the space that they're in – a
reminder of how a sofa can
change the way we see the world.

Sofa designer
Piero Lissoni

Manufacturer
Living Divani

Year designed
2020

About the sofa

The Sumo sofa, designed by Milan-based Piero Lissoni for Living Divani in 2020, exemplifies contemporary elegance despite its bold sculptural presence. Inspired by the physicality and poise of sumo wrestlers, the design combines substantial padded volumes with a light silhouette. It rests on slim, elongated wooden feet that contrast with the robust body, creating a sense of balance and sophistication. Since its launch, the Sumo sofa has gained recognition as a refined icon of modern Italian design.

About the owners

Japanese-born Yuichi Kodai runs Kodai and Associates with his Italian wife, Claudia Maggi. The architectural studio, originally founded in Kyoto and later based in Zürich, blends Eastern and Western design philosophies, with their practice also combining disciplines spanning architecture, interiors, furniture and garden design, as well as art installations. Career highlights include Kodai's work on the award-winning Kohtei Zen temple in Japan and a host of collaborative projects across Europe.

Since Yuichi Kodai is an architect who specialises in making comfortable homes for his clients, it's appropriate that his favourite sofa is located in one such project. The Japanese-born architect had admired the Sumo sofa by Italian brand Living Divani before it finally made its way into a residential project that he was working on for a client, with his wife and business partner, Claudia Maggi.

Since founding their Zürich-based studio in 2017, the duo have focused on crafting spaces that feel quiet, intentional and deeply connected to their surroundings. Their practice blends Japanese and Swiss design sensibilities, with an emphasis on residential architecture and finely crafted interiors. And while the architects can labour over details, the selection of the Sumo for this residence was – according to the couple – a no-brainer. "It feels connected to the way we work," says Kodai, explaining that it was a natural fit, both aesthetically and philosophically. With its low-slung form, slim silhouette and light-brown leather upholstery, it strongly resonated with their architectural sensibilities. "It's sleek, elegant and grounded."

Indeed, the Sumo rests closer to the floor than most contemporary sofa models, lending a subtle, almost meditative shift in perspective to those sitting on it. "You sit low and the view changes," says Kodai. "You see the sky, the horizon and it opens you up." There's a sculptural element to the piece too: seen from certain angles, particularly when approaching from the mezzanine above the living room in which the sofa is located, the Sumo brings to mind a *zabuton*. These broad, square cushions are a familiar feature of traditional Japanese interiors. "It has that same comfort," says Kodai. "A grounded feeling, but with elegance."

For both Kodai and Maggi, good proportions are essential in any piece of furniture and the Sumo is one item that gets it just right. Its slim seat cushions and low back and armrests provide a visual lightness that balances its generous scale. "It doesn't feel heavy," says Kodai. "The line that it creates from a distance is beautiful. The cushion is thin but very comfortable. There's a delicacy in the shape, a slight curve that's just right." The brown leather adds to this quiet refinement, says Kodai, before explaining that even the name of the sofa is intriguing to them. "Sumo sounds like something big and heavy," he adds. "But the design is fine and light. It's clever. It connects with the floor but with feet that lift it slightly. There's

"Sumo sounds like something big and heavy but the design is fine and light. It's clever"

a sense of elevation, as though it hovers just above the ground."

Though they haven't designed a sofa themselves, Kodai and Maggi are acutely aware of how furniture shapes the way people live. "A sofa dominates how we use a room and how we design it," says Kodai. "That's why the alignment of values between the space and its design has to be right." For the duo, a good sofa balances elegance and comfort, structure and softness. It should invite conversation, support moments of pause and feel naturally at home in the space. Photographed together on the Sumo in one of their client's homes, Kodai and Maggi can be seen embodying such an alignment: perched comfortably and quietly confident on a sofa that reflects their ethos.

21.
Ilse Crawford
On the Ilse sofa

London, UK

Sofa design can sometimes come from necessity. Ilse Crawford's namesake sofa was created as a "room within a room" for an overnight guest in her open-plan apartment. Two decades and countless refinements later, its mission remains unchanged: to provide solace and safety within.

Sofa designer
Ilse Crawford

Manufacturer
George Smith

Year designed
2005

About the sofa
The sofa that Ilse Crawford designed for British furniture maker George Smith had a long gestation period. First created in 2005 as a bespoke piece for her own open-plan living space, it went into full production a decade later and is still available today, as part of a collection including a chair, footstool and ottoman. Handmade at the George Smith factory in Northumberland in northeast England, the Ilse sofa has a distinctively high back, creating an enclosed, box-like space.

About the owner
Designer Ilse Crawford founded Studioilse in 2003, while working as the founding editor of *Elle Decoration* in the UK, which she left in 2019. She has also held roles at the Design Academy Eindhoven and is known for her human-centric approach to interiors and furniture design, prioritising wellbeing and comfort. Project highlights include the Ett Hem hotel in Stockholm, Cathay Pacific airport lounges, a collection for Ikea and Soho House in New York, all embodying her philosophy of designing for life.

"It has been through so many iterations – it's been refined and refined," says Ilse Crawford of the Ilse sofa, which she designed for Northumberland-based furniture maker George Smith. "It started life as a response to a need," says Crawford, adding that she conceived it at a time when a friend would regularly stay over in her open-plan apartment and she wanted to enable him to sleep with more privacy. "We basically designed this for him, so it became a kind of room within a room, or a box within the bigger box," says Crawford. "Since then, we've used it in loads of projects and each time it's got slightly better."

"I think that humans are much more primal than they realise on so many levels. And sofas, rather than chairs, really speak to that"

The Ilse is a large, deep sofa, with a deceptively simple design. Its relatively high back gives a cocoon-like feel. "For me, this sofa is really a sort of den," adds Crawford, noting that the first bespoke version was created in 2005. It didn't make it into wider production for another decade. The specific model currently in Crawford's Bermondsey home and workplace is more than a decade old and ageing extremely well. "It's the real deal, with horsehair and cotton and wool. We didn't want to use foam." The sofa is upholstered in linen, though it can also be finished in mohair velvet ("very robust").

Nowadays the Ilse sofa comes with detachable sides for increased ease of delivery into domestic spaces; it now also has a lower back and the seat has crept up in height. "We all love the aesthetics of the low seat," she says. "But the reality is that once you have slightly older people in the mix, the low-slung sofa is not popular."

Crawford talks about how, in her work, there is a need to think beyond obvious metrics and simply ticking the functional or regulatory requirements of a design. And that rings especially true for a sofa. "Some of the unmeasurable values that we wanted to integrate here were feelings of safety, privacy, care, integrity, robustness and dependability, and a sense of time slowing down inside the magic space," she says. "All contained within very measurable dimensions. Tricky."

This understanding and awareness of the human and emotional dimensions in design has run throughout Crawford's work since she founded Studioilse in 2003. Projects ranging from first-class airport lounges to therapeutic schools for children with emotional challenges have all been built on these holistic principles. "While we do the insides of buildings, we use architecture, interior design, journalism and film-making to make buildings that, for me, are living organisms," says Crawford. "The way the world is right now, it's very functional and very structured in silos. It doesn't really talk about the properties of things." As to whether the Ilse sofa is now finished? "I think nothing's ever finished, right? It's finished for now. But life will change, so let's see."

22.

Angie Brooks &
Lawrence Scarpa
*On a custom-made
sofa*

Los Angeles, USA

Angie Brooks and Lawrence
Scarpa's sofa isn't really
furniture – it's architecture
with cushions. Built into their
Venice Beach living room, it has
hosted sleepovers and reading
marathons while surviving kids,
cats and even a "no jumping
from the landing" rule.

Sofa designer
Brooks + Scarpa

Manufacturer
Custom installation by
Cameo Chair

Year designed
2005

About the sofa
Spanning six metres in
length and nearly a metre
deep, this custom sofa,
built on a cherrywood
frame and upholstered
in Knoll's textured Knot
Umber fabric, reflects
Brooks + Scarpa's
commitment to crafting
furniture as thoughtfully
as buildings. The piece's
deep proportions and
queen-sized dimensions
make it equally suited for
lounging, sleeping and
entertaining. The sofa is
built into the geometry of
the house and draws on
the modernist legacy of
architect Paul Rudolph,
who influenced Lawrence
Scarpa's early career.

About the owner
Angie Brooks and
Lawrence Scarpa,
principals of Brooks +
Scarpa, are renowned for
their socially conscious
and environmentally
innovative architecture.
The partners in business
and life are based in
Los Angeles and Fort
Lauderdale, Florida.

Portfolio highlights
include the Southern
Utah Museum of Art,
Leed Platinum certified
Cherokee Studios in Los
Angeles, and their own
residence, Solar Umbrella
house, a mid-century
home remodelled using
active and passive solar
design strategies to enable
the house to function
independently of the
electrical grid.

For architects Angie Brooks and Lawrence Scarpa, design is never separate from life – it's shaped by it, lived in and constantly reimagined. That ethos radiates from the heart of their Venice Beach home in Los Angeles, a place where the boundaries between architecture, furniture and landscape blur. And nowhere is that clearer than in the sunken couch: a six-metre-long sculptural form that functions as furniture, gathering place and architectural statement all at once.

"It's not even really a couch," says Scarpa. "It's a part of the house. It's integrated structurally and spatially." Built during a major renovation that tripled the size of the original bungalow, the couple explain that they always wanted to create their own sofa for the space. "We never even thought of getting a store-bought couch," adds Scarpa. "You can't buy one at this length, so why not build one into the space?"

Designed to host everything from casual afternoon hangouts to sleepovers (four people can comfortably get some shuteye here), the couch is a microcosm of the home's larger philosophy – one built around flexibility, durability and a deep connection to nature. "This is the social heart of the house," adds Brooks. "It's where people gather, stretch out, nap, talk. It's where we watch sports matches, where we read. It's got bookshelves tucked into the ends, vents coming from underneath and storage beneath the platform."

Over the years, the couch has seen its share of action, from kids launching themselves off it to a cat scratching the fabric beyond repair, prompting a full reupholstering. "We had to set some ground rules but there's only one that stuck," Scarpa says with a smile. "No jumping from the landing above."

This prohibition on leaping from a height is partly driven by the fact that the living room's floor has been sunken by nearly a metre from that of the original home, a move that allowed the architects to gain precious ceiling height while staying within Venice Beach's tight planning regulations. Front sliding doors and clerestory windows on either side create powerful cross-ventilation, making air conditioning unnecessary. "We tried to make it as passive as possible," says Scarpa. "You open the sliders on the upper windows and you feel the air just come through."

As with everything in the Brooks-Scarpa residence, the sofa is a blend of practicality and poetic detail. Built from hardy, low-maintenance materials, it's upholstered

"We had to set some ground rules but there's only one that stuck: no jumping from the landing above"

in a natural-toned fabric that works with the broader material palette of rusted steel and exposed concrete. More broadly, it's a reflection of the earthy, environmentally minded focus of the home: a raised canopy shades the south-facing façade; stormwater is directed into a hidden gravel basin; solar panels – some now 20 years old – still work overhead, powering the building.

"It's like a cave that's open. There's something instinctual about it," says Scarpa, reflecting on the home and the space that they have deliberately carved out for its sofa. "This isn't just a couch – it's part of our life," adds Brooks. "It's where our kid grew up, where our friends gather, where the light comes in just right in the morning. It's a place to be."

23.
Tosin Oshinowo
On the Aidan sofa

Cambridge, Massachusetts, USA

Tosin Oshinowo is always on the move. The Nigerian architect is frequently bouncing between places such as Lagos, London, Milan, Venice and Sharjah. She has also had an extended stint in Cambridge, Massachusetts, as one of Harvard University's Loeb fellows. And it's here, in a house shared with other fellows near the academic institution's campus, that she talks about the Aidan sofa. "This is a remarkable sofa with an illustrious history," says Oshinowo. "All manner of people have sat on this couch since I've been here. We've had Latin American mayors, Harvard professors, poets – even Guinness world-record holders."

Oshinowo's namesake studio is known for working on public and private projects in Africa, both commercial and residential – and for curating exhibitions and designing installations, including at the Sharjah Architecture Triennial and the Venice Biennale. It means that it's hard to pinpoint exactly where Oshinowo is based and that she frequently has to make other people's spaces her own, but that doesn't create a sense of displacement. Her place in Cambridge is but one example of this.

"It's not my couch, though it certainly could be," says Oshinowo, adding that despite being an old, out-of-production model from Illinois-based company Crate & Barrel, the sofa feels modern and welcoming. "It's well suited to the kind of hosting that we do for our Loeb dinners," says Oshinowo. "The sofa's posture is strong and regimented but it's comfortable. When the dining has finished, people drift into the room with a glass of wine and that's when the real conversation begins."

The seat has helped to enhance Oshinowo's work. "Choices to select a sofa like this seem small but they have a major impact. People confidently speak their mind when they really feel comfortable."

But who was the record holder that graced the couch? "That was Tunde Onakoya, a fellow Nigerian who played the world's longest chess game. He did it over 58 hours in Times Square," says Oshinowo. "I bet he was wishing he'd been sitting on a sofa like this."

Sofa designer
Crate & Barrel

Manufacturer
Crate & Barrel

Year designed
2014

About the sofa
The Aidan sofa by Crate & Barrel – a much-loved furniture and homeware company with stores across the US and Canada – is a model from the 2010s and references classic mid-century design. With clean lines, slim track arms and distinctive tufted cushions, it looks sleek while offering visual and physical comfort. Its hardwood frame adds longevity, making it ideal for both upright seating and relaxed lounging.

About the owner
Tosin Oshinowo founded her Lagos-based practice in 2013, after earning a master's degree from the Bartlett School of Architecture in London and working at the likes of SOM and OMA. Her projects include the Ngarannam village in Nigeria, a housing project for displaced people, and the Commonwealth War Graves Commission's Freetown Memorial in Sierra Leone.

24.
Jasper Morrison
On the Jota sofa

London, UK

Jasper Morrison is known for his designs that seek to support daily life through simplicity. His own Jota sofa, which he designed, embodies this philosophy: it's an understated piece that is a practical perch, whose strong lines create an atmosphere of clarity and confidence.

Sofa designer
Jasper Morrison

Manufacturer
Fredericia

Year designed
2024

About the sofa

Jasper Morrison's 2024 collaboration with family-owned Danish furniture company Fredericia (established in 1911) produced the Jota sofa, a seating system that exhibits clean lines, exceptional craftsmanship and comfort. Handmade in the company's Svendborg workshop, the Jota comes in two sizes, along with a matching lounge chair. Built around a wooden frame and mounted on oak legs, the cushions are filled with down and foam granulate mix and finished with French stitching.

About the owner

Since his career began in the mid-1980s, British designer Jasper Morrison's work has returned to the idea of the "super normal", the notion that ordinary, everyday objects, often those that have been designed anonymously, perform better than their designed counterparts. His aesthetic has been applied to everything from public transportation systems and shops to art galleries, furniture, lighting and tableware. His extensive portfolio is characterised by a quiet elegance and a focus on essential needs.

"I'm not a big fan of the trend for massive, deep, L-shaped sofas that take up most of the room, offering the idea of comfort rather than the real thing," says Jasper Morrison. The London-based designer is explaining the rationale behind his choice of sofa. But where most of us must filter through an endless selection of makes, models, sizes and styles of furniture to find the one that is just

"Maybe that is the real function of a sofa – just to allow yourself the feeling of not going anywhere?"

right, Morrison was able to design and create this sofa, named Jota, himself.

"Perhaps I'm best known for promoting the idea of 'super normal'," says Morrison. "Super normal came about through noticing that objects that perform best have qualities beyond their purely visible and obviously functional ones." Jota is a case in point: a two-seater sofa created for Danish furniture brand Fredericia, it combines Scandinavian heritage with modern sophistication. "I designed Jota to be more homely and offer a more practical comfort without taking up too much space," he says. "The quality that Fredericia's craftsmanship brought to the design makes it something special, even though its form isn't trying to show off at all."

The deceptive simplicity of the Jota conforms to a certain aesthetic that runs through Morrison's many projects. His portfolio includes the orb-like Glo Ball series of lamps for Flos, the Air Chair for Magis and the gently rounded Soft Modular Sofa for Vitra. "They are probably linked by an inability to suffer a bad atmosphere," says Morrison. "For me it's all about making the atmosphere better, giving it a sense of simplicity and ease, so I make the same effort with each project to try to uncomplicate things and as far as possible reduce them to their essence."

As with Morrison's previous sofas, the Jota came with familiar challenges. "I have designed quite a few and the difficulty with each project is to give them enough of a sense of what a sofa is," he says. "They need to occupy a room in the best way a sofa can, providing the right feeling of comfort."

It's an atmosphere that the Jota sofa is, according to Morrison, cultivating in his own home. A newer arrival to the residence, the designer says that he's still trying to find it a perfect berth. "It moves around a bit, looking for the place where it belongs," says Morrison. "But it's holding up well. I haven't detected any signs of wear. We're a family of five, so it gets used well. 'No food' is the only rule."

The result? A sofa that works perfectly as a place to be when his working life – split between Tokyo, London and St Leonards, on England's south coast – finally comes to a pause. "As I move around rather a lot, it gives me a sense of finally coming to a stop," he says. "Maybe that is the real function of a sofa – just to allow yourself the feeling of not going anywhere."

25.
Rodrigo Bravo
On the Can sofa

Santiago, Chile

The Can sofa that furnishes Rodrigo Bravo's home shows that there is a certain power in restraint. Produced by Danish firm Hay, the flat-pack design is a showcase in elegant efficiency, with a pared-back appearance that allows people to take precedence.

Sofa designer
Ronan & Erwan
Bouroullec

Manufacturer
Hay

Year designed
2016

About the sofa
Can's creators, the
fraternal Parisian design
duo, Ronan & Erwan
Bouroullec, regard
their design as deeply
enabling for the owner,
who can choose from
a selection of sizes. On
offer is a one-seater club
chair, a two-seater sofa
and a three-seater sofa.
Manufactured by Danish
furniture powerhouse
Hay, it arrives flat-packed,
stripping away complexity
and offering a simple,
accessible and versatile

lounge solution that
reflects the Bouroullecs'
pursuit of elegant efficiency
and practicality.

About the owner
Based in Santiago, Chilean
industrial designer Rodrigo
Bravo heads his namesake
studio, established in
2005. Bravo's practice
spans interior architecture,
furniture and product
design, and is driven by
an approach rooted in
understanding materials
and production processes.
This experimental yet

common-sense approach
to design allows Bravo to
create unique solutions
that reflect distinct making
processes and cultures.

In 2020, at the height of the pandemic, Rodrigo Bravo swapped his home for his studio. At the time, the Chilean designer and his family lived in a modest apartment in central Santiago, while he had run his studio, also called Bravo, from a more spacious property on the capital's periphery. Lockdowns made his family place greater value on the domestic environment. "We needed more space and the studio building had a very nice garden," says Bravo. "In the end we said, 'why don't we live here?'"

The contents of the two properties were swapped around; the only thing that remained at the studio was the three-seater Can sofa designed by Ronan & Erwan Bouroullec (*see page 170*) and produced by Danish brand Hay, which now forms the family home's centrepiece. Bravo says that he was partly drawn to the sofa because it has the same name as the brilliant, mid-century German krautrock band. However, the Can's real pull lies in its simple, elegant efficiency, which appeals to Bravo's design sensibilities. "It comes flat-packed and is very easy to assemble," says the designer. "It can be assembled in 20 minutes; it's fantastic that you can build such a complex structure so quickly."

The sofa's near-poetic lack of ornamentation is a testament to the Bouroullec brothers, who worked through a series of prototypes, gradually reducing its form to a sleek final result. It consists of a steel frame upon which rests a tent-like canvas cover, which in turn retains a set of cushions. It's a combination that Bravo says is both industrial and emotive. "I love how the structure stretches the fabric – it reminds me of functional construction processes from the Second World War," he says. "It's also a very emotional work of design. Simple things can bring out certain feelings."

This emotive atmosphere makes the sofa the perfect backdrop for a family. Bravo explains that there are almost no rules surrounding the sofa. "Well, the only rule is that we are together and we connect," he says. "I sit on it with my children; we play board games or work on school projects and, after dinner, when they are in bed, I take my shoes off and read on it."

Can certainly seems like an excellent choice for a person unencumbered by the desire for visual or social elaboration or embellishment. And, while Bravo is happy with his French-designed, Danish-produced sofa, he adds that he draws professional inspiration from pre-Columbian sculptures, as well as the geology

"This sofa can be assembled from flatpack in 20 minutes; it's fantastic that you can build such a complex structure so quickly"

and landscape of his native Chile. As such, he says that if he were forced to choose another for his home, he'd select something currently non-existent but based on a fellow countryman's beautifully simplistic work. "What I would like is a sofa version of the Puzzle lounge chair designed by Chilean architect Juan Baixas," he says. "It's a fully assembled piece, made of wood. It's a beautiful, light and slender object."

His vision for both his current and future sofa is a reminder that, while the furniture in our home might change, a singular outlook can remain. For Bravo, that's one that prioritises unfussy utility and emotional resonance.

26.
Eric Owen Moss
On the Theatre sofa

Los Angeles, USA

It pays to break rules. Architect Eric Owen Moss's unorthodox buildings have proved this – and his furniture does too. Built into his off-kilter home, his curved and sloped sofas fit walls that refuse right angles. It shows that typical geometries aren't the only way to find comfort.

Sofa designer
Eric Owen Moss

Manufacturer
Custom installation by DMC Made

Year designed
2022

About the sofa
The home's theatre (*pictured above*), and symposium seating embody a synthesis of geometry, craft and comfort. In the theatre, three rows of terraced seating are carved into a bowl-shaped floor, itself formed by a curve in the building envelope. Baltic birch plywood, continuous from the upper floors, creates a unified material palette. Custom foam cushions conform to the contours of the bowl, resulting in an amphitheatre-like experience softened by large throw pillows for flexible lounging.

About the owner
Eric Owen Moss founded his namesake studio in 1973. The Los Angeles-based architect is renowned for his sculptural, provocative, deconstructivist style that challenges conventional design norms. His studio is most renowned for transforming Culver City's Hayden Tract into an architectural wonderland; key projects in this Los Angeles neighbourhood include the Samitaur Tower, a tilting, steel-clad observation tower, and Stealth, a building with distinct angular forms. His (W)rapper office building in Los Angeles, with its twisting façade, is another example of Moss's ability to create structures that define and shape an urban environment.

Eric Owen Moss is not a typical architect. His sofa is not a typical sofa – or, in this case, two custom-made sofas, built to fit within the off-kilter contours of his home in Santa Monica Canyon, where virtually no surface is straight. The house was made to fit the furniture and the furniture was made to perfectly fit the house.

The sofas can be found defining the first floor's two living spaces. In one room, dubbed the *symposium* (a name that Moss says refers more to a few friends sitting around having a beer than to any formal Socratic exchange), a curved sofa hugs the irregular geometry of the wall. The other room is the *theatre*, where a sloped floor – cantilevering out from the house's envelope – supports a tiered series of cushions that form a built-in amphitheatre; sitting perpendicular to this are two more standard-looking sofas.

Both spaces and sofas are well used. His son, Miller – an American Football quarterback – often takes over the Theatre sofa with his teammates, watching sports and playing video games. "They're twice as big as me," says Moss with a shrug. "They hang around, they have coffee and they're gone." In addition to hosting friends, Moss uses the Symposium sofa as a perch to survey his wildly eclectic neighbourhood – a stretch that mixes million-dollar homes with a concrete-lined canal and a jumble of oddball businesses.

"It's not the image you think of when you hear Santa Monica Canyon," he says. "This is the flatlands of Los Angeles County, where you've got a hunk of concrete in the canal, which is not particularly sanitised, and a lot of traffic, noise and neon. As you go up the canyon, it gets fancier."

Inside, Moss's home is a continuation of this unruly streetscape. Nothing is static. Walls bend, floors lean, the furniture adapts to subtle angles. The symposium sofa, for instance, isn't just tucked against the wall – it mirrors its curvature, its tilt, its refusal to stay still. Even the pillows are trapezoidal, subtly customised to rest against walls that never meet at right angles. The house is deeply personal and its furniture – mostly designed by Moss, some bespoke, some adapted from existing furniture – tells part of that story. The pieces echo the home's movement between forms, with

"There are imperfections in the house. Places where the underlayment didn't quite work or the sticks didn't quite align. But we want to see that"

a plan that morphs from a rooftop rectangle into a guitar-shaped ground floor. Between those two layers, the building shifts, curves and transforms.

"There are imperfections," says Moss. "Places where the underlayment didn't quite work or the sticks didn't quite align. But we want to see that too." A resin-like skin coats the building and is left raw like a green industrial rooftop. It's not about perfection. It's about process, experimentation, play.

Is the home a refuge? Moss resists that label. "Refuge would be more to withdraw from the world," he says. Instead, the house remains in dialogue with the dynamic streetscape and the ever-shifting use of its spaces. The sofas, like the house, are not about retreating but rather staying engaged, curious and open-ended.

27.
Daniel Libeskind
On the Big C sofa

New York, USA

Buying on impulse can be good. A case in point is architect Daniel Libeskind's sculptural sofa by Pierre Paulin – a spontaneous purchase that proved to be transformative. This distinctive piece sparked a complete home reorganisation and became a central element in his life.

Sofa designer
Pierre Paulin

Manufacturer
Louis Vuitton

Year designed
1977

About the sofa
Pierre Paulin's Big C sofa, designed in 1977, perfectly encapsulates his revolutionary approach to seating. The French designer's ethos of merging organic shapes with industrial innovation is evident in its construction: a seamless, upholstered form created by stretching vibrant fabric over a hidden timber frame and plush foam. The result is a sofa that transcends mere furniture, becoming a sculptural statement that prioritises profound comfort and optimistic modern aesthetics, securing its place as an enduring design classic in the canon of sofas.

About the owner
Born in Poland, Daniel Libeskind moved to the US when he was a teenager and studied architecture at New York's Cooper Union. He established his namesake studio in Berlin in 1989 and has since become a seminal figure in deconstructivist architecture. His style is defined by sharp angles, fragmented geometries and powerful symbolic narratives, often explaining themes of memory and history. Key projects include the Jewish Museum Berlin, the master plan for the World Trade Center site in New York and the Denver Art Museum, all embodying his distinctive, emotive style.

"It was a complete impulse buy," says Daniel Libeskind, who purchased the sofa for his Manhattan apartment on a whim. "I couldn't believe it when I saw the object," adds the architect, who splits his time between New York and Berlin and spotted the couch in question while visiting Louis Vuitton's Design Miami showcase in 2014. Here, 18 unreleased or out-of-production works by the late French experimental designer Pierre Paulin – including a long, gently curving sofa called the Big C – had been created as a limited collection by the French fashion house.

The designs had remained mostly unproduced in Paulin's lifetime due to financial issues, existing instead as models, sketches and plans. These were on show for the first time after Paulin's widow, Maïa, approached Louis Vuitton about a partnership. "Towards

"I saw that the sofa – unlike other pieces in the collection – still hadn't been purchased and I thought, 'You're kidding me?' So, I bought it"

the end of the day, I saw that the sofa – unlike other pieces in the collection – still hadn't been purchased and I thought, 'You're kidding me?'" says Libeskind, laughing. "So, I bought it – but without consideration of the size, the scale, the complexity of getting it up a building in New York." Installing this almost four-metre-long lounge into his apartment building in the

Tribeca neighbourhood in Manhattan was a challenge but once it was installed the effect was immediate.

"It's amazing what a great piece of furniture can do," says Libeskind, whose sofa now takes pride of place alongside a complementary Paulin-designed coffee table. "It is an element of space. It's like a major renovation of your house."

The sofa was part of a series of designs that Paulin created in an attempt to transcend room limitations, reflecting his research into changing, nomadic living habits. Its introduction into Libeskind's home conflicted with the existing rectilinear modernist forms that populated the space, prompting a complete reshuffle of his furniture. "I love Mies and Le Corbusier but their pieces had to be exported to my office because the Paulin is big enough to replace a few pieces of furniture," says Libeskind. "It's a bold piece but it's not aggressive, occupying the space with great authority."

Part of the ongoing appeal of the Big C, Libeskind adds, is the fact that its style can't be readily defined. "It's not designed in a certain style but it has a bold and formal element, an unusual red-purple colour, an unexpected form that was clearly drawn by hand," says Libeskind. The distinctive, deeply curved, C-shaped form invites an intimate lounging experience, gently turning those sitting on it to face one another. "It's remarkable that all my kids and grandkids can all sit on a single piece of furniture," says Libeskind, before adding that the sofa has, above all, transformed the atmosphere of his home. "What makes a great sofa is not only the comfort but what it looks like when you're not sitting on it. It's about the views that you get of it from different angles – looking down on it, looking across the room, looking for a distant horizon. I see it as a sculpture."

28.
Yuko Nagayama
On the Sax sofa

Tokyo, Japan

Yuko Nagayama's sleek modular sofa could hardly be more different from the formal one that she remembers from her childhood in Tokyo's Asagaya neighbourhood. "The house I was born in was a traditional Japanese house," says the architect. "There was a large sofa on the tatami floor that was mostly used when we had guests."

Nagayama's current home is nothing like that old house. Hers is an airy renovated apartment on top of a 50-year-old block that she shares with her husband – the artist Akira Fujimoto – and their two children. There are big windows, a sunny terrace and an expansive Tokyo vista with houses, train lines and, rising majestically in the distance, Mount Fuji.

As with many Tokyo apartments, there isn't much furniture: a table that Nagayama designed for one of her buildings, Maruni chairs by Jasper Morrison (*see page 90*), a long bench desk facing Mount Fuji and a Sax sofa designed by Spanish designer Rafa García. A simple, boxy form, the sofa takes pride of place in the family's open living, eating and sleeping area. "It reminds me of a *koagari*, a raised *tatami* platform," says Nagayama. "You can sit on different parts – on the back, on the arm, on the seat."

Unlike the one in her childhood home, Nagayama's sofa is not reserved for guests only. "My kids basically dominate the sofa these days," says Nagayama. "It's their territory now." She adds that she mostly uses the Sax at night-time when she sketches, with

some of her best ideas – such as her design for the Panasonic Group Pavilion at the Osaka 2025 Expo – occurring on the sofa.

It's a combination that means Nagayama's Sax sofa has withstood some heavy use over the years (there was one alarming run-in with slime) but the dark Kvadrat fabric is very forgiving. "I've been thinking about changing the sofa recently but my kids love this style," says Nagayama. "We've had this one since we moved in here, so it's part of our family story."

Sofa designer
Rafa García

Manufacturer
Sancal

Year designed
2005

About the sofa
Murcia-based furniture firm Sancal was founded in 1973 with a mission to bring designs by both Spanish designers and a roster of international talent to their collections. Rafa Garcia has authored countless designs for the brand, including the Sax. Launched in 2005, Sax has deep cushions and an understated presence with a clean, precise silhouette, supported by a robust structure of FSC-certified wood. It can be customised with a number of different components and finished with a choice of fabrics.

About the owner
Yuko Nagayama is one of Japan's most prominent architects, having worked on projects including the 48-storey Tokyu Kabukicho Tower and the renovation of a historic *ryokan* inn in Gunma. She has also created products including the P Sofa for Tokyo-based firm By Interiors, which is designed to sit on *tatami* mats without leaving a mark and is scaled to fit the size of Japanese homes.

29.
Tatiana Bilbao
On the Soft Dream sofa

Mexico City, Mexico

Architects often talk about their work's longevity; Tatiana Bilbao extends this to her Flexform sofa, which has endured five children and countless Christmas mornings. The architect embraces its weathered look – a reminder that furniture comes alive through human interaction.

Sofa designer
Antonio Citterio

Manufacturer
Flexform

Year designed
2010

About the sofa
When Italian furniture company Flexform created the Soft Dream sofa in 2010, it was the latest in a long series of collaborations with Antonio Citterio and part of a "quest to design a sofa that encourages dreaming". Made to be lightweight and versatile, the sofa is constructed from a few simple elements: the cast metal feet support a cowhide-upholstered base, piled with goose-down-filled cushions, while the armrests come in high and low versions for versatility.

About the owner
Tatiana Bilbao's architectural practice, based in Mexico City, spans a diverse range of project typologies, ranging from low-cost housing prototypes to large cultural institutions, master plans and furniture, often integrating local materials and building traditions. As the founder of Tatiana Bilbao Estudio, she leads a team of creatives with a process that emphasises collaboration and hand-drawn processes, leading to impactful and contextually rich architecture. Her practice has completed buildings in Mexico, the US, France, Germany and China.

The focal point of Tatiana Bilbao's home is a huge Soft Dream sofa from Flexform. Designed in 2010 by Antonio Citterio, with goose-down cushions, rough-hewn linen-blend fabric and slender metal feet, it has withstood more than a decade of heavy use from Bilbao's family (with her husband, they have five children between them). "It's big, low and comfortable. I find it very beautiful," says Bilbao. "We try to keep it clean. However, we're almost giving up. We use it so much that it has faded but I like that."

The Mexico City-based architect's professional life has long been focused on how physical environments and humans interact. "The straightforward answer is that I'm an architect," she says. "But the majority of the time I believe that I'm not. I operate in a totally different manner to most. I try to enable processes for the creation of space with and around people."

This human-centred approach has run through Bilbao's work since the 2004 founding of her namesake studio. While best

"When the time arrived, I knew exactly which sofa I wanted. It was a very short decision-making process"

known in the academic world for her teaching and theories on housing, she is associated in her native Mexico City with her work on the Culiacan Botanical Garden, the Sea of Cortez Research Center in Mazatlán and her many international projects. Often her process prioritises hand drawing and collage over digital methods. "The truth is that I don't think I work," she says.

"I live it 24 hours a day, 365 days a year." While much of this time is spent in transit (Bilbao estimates that she is away for 120 to 150 days per year), she is solidly grounded in her family home in the Mexican capital's Polanco district, close to her studio in neighbouring Juárez. "We live in an apartment building from 1946 that was built by Mario Pani, the architect of modern Mexico," she says of the residence that she has lived in since 2006. Significantly, the building also has a large garden (a rarity for an apartment in such a central neighbourhood of the city).

For Bilbao, the sofa at the heart of this home is intertwined with family memories. "My daughter was just born when we got it and all of our kids have grown up on this couch," says Bilbao. "It's pretty big, so we can sit together; it's the place where we have Christmas, where someone naps during the day and it's where children would jump in and out – the three oldest have boyfriends and girlfriends now, so those come in too."

In short, the sofa is a welcoming space, reflecting her attitude to both hosting and her professional practice. "We ask everyone to take care but I'm not so picky," says Bilbao. "I'm not the kind of architect who needs to keep spaces pristine. Buildings evolve with their users and that's how architecture stays alive. That's the same way that I use my space."

The impact of such an approach is the formation of a deep relationship between the user and the space or object, as evidenced by the Soft Dream. "If I were to buy a new sofa now, I would buy the same one – so let's see how it ages with us. It has a lot of life left," says Bilbao. "Maybe my kids will have it."

30.
Keiji Ashizawa
On the A-SOI sofa

Tokyo, Japan

Can a seat be a bridge between Japan's tatami culture and Western sofa traditions? Architect Keiji Ashizawa's sofa is designed to do just that. It can be used as a support when sitting on the floor and as a fine seat in its own right – perfect for lounging, as a party perch and more.

Sofa designer
Keiji Ashizawa &
Norm Architects

Manufacturer
Karimoku Case

Year designed
2019

About the sofa
The A-SOI sofa, designed by Keiji Ashizawa for Karimoku Case, epitomises understated Japanese elegance. Part of a collaborative project blending architecture and furniture, this sofa reflects Ashizawa's "honest design" ethos, celebrating natural materials and meticulous craftsmanship. It features a clean, low-slung profile and a subtly exposed solid wood frame. With generous, plush cushions, it offers exceptional comfort and an inviting presence, striking the balance between a traditional Western sofa form and Japanese culture.

About the owner
Japanese designer Keiji Ashizawa graduated from Yokohama National University and established Keiji Ashizawa Design in Tokyo in 2005 after a stint working in a steel workshop. It was an educational background that led to a hands-on approach to architecture, furniture and product design, with Ashizawa prioritising natural materials, simplicity and functionality in his work. Ashizawa also leads Ishinomaki Laboratory, founded after the 2011 east Japan tsunami. This workshop creates durable, simple furniture from Japanese timber, empowering the community in its ongoing recovery.

"Japan doesn't really have a sofa culture, like in the West," says Keiji Ashizawa. "We have a tatami culture which is amazing because you can sleep, sit and eat dinner on them." The globally renowned designer knows a thing or two about creating furniture rooted in Japanese traditions. A case in point is his A-SOI sofa, which takes pride of place in his home: low to the ground and with deep seats, it is, in essence, an elevated tatami.

"In Japan, people still tend to sit on the ground in front of sofas. I designed this one so you can rest your arm on it and with seats deep enough to sleep on," says Ashizawa. "I didn't want to design a 'sofa' sofa, so it sits somewhere between Japan and Europe."

Created in 2019 for the renovation of apartments in the Kinuta Terrace complex in Tokyo's Setagaya district, it was one of the

"I have a cat and a very small dog and they both jump up on the couch. It's the most comfortable space in the communal areas"

first pieces of furniture produced as part of the Karimoku Case programme. A collaboration launched in partnership with the furniture brand Karimoku, Copenhagen-based Norm Architects and Ashizawa's own design studio, the initiative saw the firms collaborating on an architectural project for which they designed everything from the building and interiors to the furniture. At the Kinuta Terrace, this involved a renovation placing the building's interiors in closer contact with the verdant courtyard. This is reflected in the 12 tailor-made furniture pieces designed for the project, with a philosophy of harmonising indoor spaces with the natural environment.

Part of meeting that brief entailed using a very simple material palette. The sofa features an oak frame and has a notably low profile – designed to enhance the spaciousness of the room that it is placed in, while its clever multifunctional armrests double as pillows, inviting daybed-like lounging. "When we created these small apartments in Kinuta, we didn't want to use many materials or colours, so that the furniture would be very calm but very gorgeous," says Ashizawa. "I try to design honestly. This means minimalism – for the sofa, that's a simple construction, with the cushions easy to assemble and disassemble."

Now the sofa has found itself a home in Ashizawa's own compact residence. The architect has just moved into a smaller apartment close to his office, with the sofa becoming the focal point of the living room for the whole family. "I have a cat and a very small dog – Penelope the pomeranian – and they both jump up on the couch," says Ashizawa. "It's the most comfortable space in the communal areas. After work it's a very relaxing spot: sometimes I have to fight to stay awake when I'm reading or watching the news."

Also speaking to the success of the case-study initiative is that this isn't the only A-SOI sofa that Ashizawa owns. "There is one in this apartment, one at my house on the edge of the city and one at my company's guesthouse," says Ashizawa with a smile. "I tried to buy a different sofa but this somehow feels the most comfortable. I like that it's wide, that it has depth and when we have a problem we can always change the upholstery."

31.
Thomas Hildebrand
On the DS-80 daybed

Zürich, Switzerland

Thomas Hildebrand's workplace, a former hydroelectric plant, is a dialogue between past and present. His 1969 De Sede daybed bears the patina of decades of use, while the bespoke timber wall that it's set against proves his philosophy that outstanding design deserves reinvention.

Sofa designer
De Sede

Manufacturer
De Sede

Year designed
1969

About the sofa
The DS-80 daybed, introduced by Swiss manufacturer De Sede, is an enduring icon of relaxed luxury. Designed by De Sede's in-house creative team, it features a distinctive, low-slung profile. Its narrow, high-quality seat has a patchwork leather construction, resting atop a frame of filigree wooden slats. This piece exemplifies the manufacturer's mastery of leather craftsmanship; the brand evolved from a saddlery workshop and is renowned for its meticulously handcrafted sofas and seating.

About the owner
Thomas Hildebrand founded his namesake Zürich-based practice in 2007, which is recognised for an architectural style that prioritises precise detailing and a thoughtful response to site and programme. The result? Projects that are impactful, robust and enduring. Key works include a number of residential projects – many of them noted for their refined concrete finishes and wood interior details – and a sports centre in Sargans near the border with Liechtenstein, where a lightweight wooden façade strikes a balance between aesthetics and function.

At the back of Thomas Hildebrand's Zürich office sits a DS-80 daybed by Swiss manufacturer De Sede. Purchased on Ebay, the vintage piece produced in 1969 is upholstered in plush black leather and set on a wooden slatted base. Despite being more than five decades old, it is ageing gracefully, fitting neatly with the design narrative of Hildebrand's office – a former hydroelectric power plant that has been adapted and reimagined several times.

Today he refers to the building as being in its fifth life. And the sofa, like the office space, is a study in giving an outstanding

"You can really lie down on it. That is what makes a sofa good. You should be able to take a proper nap"

work of design new life. "You do not always need to make something new," he says, of the decision to furnish his space with the DS-80, rather than a newer sofa. "If something still works well, you keep it." Hildebrand says that part of the appeal lies in memories of De Sede furniture from his childhood, especially in the homes of design-conscious family and friends. The company, founded in 1962, has produced several Swiss classics and the DS-80 is among them. Its form is unpretentious and enduring, with no exaggerated curves or flourishes. It relies instead on solid materials and clean lines to make a point.

In the office, the daybed is used casually and often. There are no rules. It is a place for meetings, reading or the occasional rest. "You can really lie down on it," says Hildebrand. "That is what makes a sofa good. You should be able to take a proper nap." Over time, the leather has softened and darkened. The patina, he says, is one of its best features – a surface that tells the story of time and use.

Though he has not designed a sofa himself, Hildebrand says that he knows what he wants from one: it should be well made, comfortable and flexible, suited not only for sitting but for stretching out and slowing down. The DS-80 meets all those criteria and does so without demanding attention. Indeed, its humility allows the daybed to sit gently alongside one of Hildebrand's works: a timber wall composed of identically milled wooden elements that now serves as a room divider and acoustic buffer.

The wooden structure was originally developed for a 2022 exhibition – *Touch Wood* by Gramazio Kohler Research at ETH – that Hildebrand co-curated. After two years in storage, the wall found its way into his studio: it fits perfectly, bringing tactility and warmth to the space. What was once an exhibition centrepiece now finds a new life in the office – together, the daybed and the wall form a quiet dialogue between past and present. One is a piece of Swiss design heritage from the 1960s; the other a contemporary experiment in pattern and repetition. Both are reused. Both remain beautiful. For Hildebrand, it is this balance that matters.

32.
Nifemi Marcus-Bello
On the Äpplaryd sofa

Lagos, Nigeria

An advocate of transparency in production, Nifemi Marcus-Bello found comfort and clarity in this flat-pack sofa. Acquired via a transatlantic journey and now taking pride of place in his living room, it serves as a hub for his family – the perfect spot for resting and reflecting.

Sofa designer
Maja Ganszyniec

Manufacturer
Ikea

Year designed
2021

About the sofa
The Äpplaryd sofa was designed by Polish-born Maja Ganszyniec, who studied in London and established her studio in Warsaw in 2013. Her commitment to combining sustainability with craft can be seen in the Äpplaryd, with its signature steel frame, slim legs and a quiet silhouette that can be configured to two, three or four seats, making for an adaptable accompaniment to living spaces of any style.

About the owner
Lagos-born and based Nifemi Marcus-Bello is recognised as one of the creatives shaping Nigeria's design scene. His practice spans continents, striking a balance between industry and craftsmanship, with the city of Lagos as a major source of inspiration. He employs a diverse design language, paying homage to both the old and contemporary Nigeria in his work, which includes furniture, installations, sculpture and products.

"Ikea has always been an interesting company that I've admired from afar," says designer Nifemi Marcus-Bello. "It's not perfect but I like its transparency on the production and design process of objects." The founder of Lagos-based Nmbello Studio is an ardent fan of the flat-pack specialist's Äppalryd sofa. He first spotted the simple piece on a trip to one of the Swedish furniture giant's shops in London, where he found himself pleasantly surprised: the Scandinavian-designed three-seater was incredibly comfortable and fulfilled his requirements. "A good sofa, once you sink in, should make you feel like you never want to get off of it," says Marcus-Bello, who studied in the UK and is known for his distinctive style that blends past and present narratives of West African migration and identity, interweaving colourful Nigerian artefacts with bold contemporary forms. "When I bought it, we didn't yet have an Ikea in Lagos, so I had to go to great lengths to ship the sofa here in one piece."

Though he has never designed a sofa professionally (he's just waiting for the right client and brief), he admits that it's a potentially daunting challenge. "Sofas, by nature, are large, spatially demanding pieces that don't lend themselves easily to the kind of sculptural, object-focused storytelling that design history tends to prioritise," says Marcus-Bello, who believes that this is why these furniture pieces tend to be relegated to the background of interior spaces. "When compared to chairs, which tend to be portable, sofas are architectural in footprint."

The mass-produced Ikea sofa replaced one that he had custom-made in Lagos. "I wasn't happy with the bespoke option, but lived with it for a very long time," says Marcus-Bello. "In 2020 after spending a lot of time on the sofa, I decided to invest in a new one." The designer never works on his sofa. "I mentally associate the sofa with rest so I can never get any work done when I'm sitting on it." That's why he puts his work bag on it during the week to remove the temptation. But the plush perch really comes into its own on the weekends, when Marcus-Bello unwinds with his friends and family. Despite being based in Lagos, he spends large portions of the year on the road, with projects spanning cities from Miami to Milan, so his

"We didn't yet have an Ikea in Lagos, so I had to go to great lengths to ship the sofa here in one piece"

furniture at home needs to play a uniting role. "The sofa plays a huge role within my space and family dynamic. It is the only chair that we can all sit on at the same time."

When selecting the Äppalryd, Marcus-Bello took durability into consideration, for what is a high-traffic seat. The textured weave of the sofa is designed to resist fading and discolouration and the optional addition of a chaise longue means that users can comfortably recline. Made from Ikea's signature Lejde fabric – comprising a mixture of polyester, viscose and cotton – it has a pleasantly textured finish. But, perhaps more importantly, Marcus-Bello also considered the limited natural light of his home's interior. The sofa is slightly raised to allow light to pass underneath and is finished in a lighter fabric, to make the object feel less hefty. "The sofa is very considerate to my space and our way of life," he says. "It's ageing gracefully and it means a lot to me when I walk into the room and I see my wife and kids sitting comfortably. It's worth every penny."

33.
Rahul Mehrotra
On the Correa sofa

Mumbai, India

"When you sit on it, you feel like you're in a room. There's this sense of containment, which is very attractive and comforting," says architect Rahul Mehrotra, describing the emotions of sitting or lying on the sofa that dominates the living room of his 1920s Mumbai apartment.

Made in the late 20th century from repurposed American pinewood packing material, it sits barely 30cm off the ground, with its three sides towering above the base. "It's got very modernist lines and feels like an architectural set," says Mehrotra, connecting the furniture's aesthetic to that of its designer, Charles Correa, the late Indian architect and urban planner who championed a version of modernism that combined the design style with vernacular forms. The sofa, designed by Correa for his own home, is part of a four-piece set, including two small tables. In the early-1990s, soon after Mehrotra married Nondita, Correa's daughter, Correa gifted the set to the couple. Not surprisingly, to them the sofa represents Correa's legacy.

"Firstly, it's a reminder of Correa, his presence in our home and our lives. It is also in keeping with the way that we as a couple deal with architecture," he says, referring to the Mehrotras' love for juxtaposing the old and the new. "We like setting up this dialogue between the contemporary and the traditional, which some people call tension."

But Mehrotra is keen to stress that sitting on a sofa should be anything but tense, adding that it should be flexible and able to readily switch functions from formal to informal – something that this sofa does well.

"Growing up, our kids would sleep on it," says Mehrotra. "You can also sit on the ground – something we like doing in India – and lean on it. When we have bigger parties, people sit on the sofa while there are others who use it as a bench, with their buttocks on the beam. The beam is also wide enough that it allows you to keep objects on it, like a stack of books. Our sofa straddles the usage spectrum very well."

Sofa designer
Charles Correa

Manufacturer
Custom made

Year designed
1990

About the sofa
This bespoke sofa was designed by renowned Indian architect Charles Correa using beams of American pinewood. The wood was used in packing imported IT hardware for the Bengaluru office of technology company Tata Elxsi, which Correa was designing. While on site, he realised the potential of the material – which might have otherwise ended up in a landfill – to be repurposed into furniture, which he did for his own home.

About the owner
Rahul Mehrotra is an architect, urbanist and founder of the award-winning RMA Architects. A professor at Harvard University's Urban Planning and Design department, he promotes hands-on learning with rigorous academia – an approach he also takes at his practice. Among his designs are the Lab of the Future in Basel and the KMC corporate office in Hyderabad, exemplifying his innovative approach to sustainable and culturally resonant spaces.

34.
Mariam Issoufou
On the Strato sofa

New York, USA

Searching for a sofa suitable for her family, Mariam Issoufou settled on this L-shaped number for its comfort and (mostly) cat-friendly bouclé – a reminder that a sofa should be well used. And it's living up to the brief, with the perch the most popular reading nook in the home.

Sofa designer
Mermelada Estudio

Manufacturer
CB2

Year designed
2020

About the sofa
The Strato sectional sofa system was designed for US firm CB2 by Mermelada Estudio, a Barcelona-based design collective founded by Laura Blasco, Juanmi Juárez and Alex Estévez that specialises in product design and art direction. Drawing inspiration from 1970s Italian designs, the sofa is characterised by the plush channel tufting that creates horizontal lines that give the sofa its architectural aesthetic. It's part of a wider collection that includes armless lounge chairs, corner armchairs and two and four-seater sofas.

About the owner
Born in France, raised in Niger and educated in the US, architect Mariam Issoufou runs her namesake studio from New York and teaches at ETH in Zürich. Her practice emphasises community-focused architecture deeply rooted in local context, materials and culture. Highlights include the award-winning Hikma Religious and Secular Complex in Dandaji, and the Ellen Johnson Sirleaf Presidential Centre for Women and Development in Liberia.

When Nigerien architect Mariam Issoufou moved to her Manhattan apartment, she picked out the new sofa based on two functional considerations. "Both my daughter and I read a lot and we bond over that," she says. "I needed a sofa where we can both be fully reclined, reading together." The ideal model, then, was a large L-shape. "The other thing is that we have a cat that sheds a lots. It's white,

> ## "My daughter and I read a lot and we bond over that. I needed a sofa where we can both be fully reclined, reading"

so I matched the sofa to the cat." The family committee decided on the four-piece Strato sofa by CB2 in an off-white bouclé fabric.

Filling up the living room in a lower midtown apartment, the sofa has delivered on its intended purpose. Behind the couch is a wall-to-wall bookcase holding Issoufou's collection (her daughter has her own library in her room). "When I'm lying on the sofa, I can just turn around, grab a book and continue reading," she says. The bookworm gene has been successfully transferred: Issoufou's daughter tackled the *Harry Potter* series at six years old and is now, as a teenager, already giving recommendations to her mother. Tips have included Nigerian author Chimamanda Ngozi Adichie's *Americanah* (a National Book Critics Circle Award winner) and several Afrofuturist fantasy novels.

When not buried in a novel, Issoufou leads a busy and itinerant life. The architect, who grew up in Niamey, the Nigerien capital, now divides her time between Zürich, where she is a professor at ETH, and New York, where the studio of her namesake firm is located. The firm has landmark buildings under construction on multiple continents, with projects including a mosque and housing development in Sharjah and the Bët-bi museum in Senegal. After coming home from the office, Issoufou has a delectable method to optimise her time spent with family. On Sundays, she likes to make a huge brunch ("It's as if I'm cooking for 10," she says) and at the same time prepare meals for the week to come. With homecooked dinner in the freezer, it is easier to catch up – and stretch out on the couch – on weekday evenings.

The sofa, in short, encourages a leisurely pace in Issoufou's apartment. This is perhaps thanks to its form. Strato's creators, Barcelona-based Mermelada Estudio, drew inspiration from 1970s Italian designs, which rebelled against the strict minimalism of mid-century modernism and emphasised comfort and multifunctionality. One clear predecessor is the iconic Strips sofa by legendary mid-century designer Cini Boeri, with both lounges characterised by soft horizontal lines. Importantly for Issoufou, Mermelada Estudio finished Strato with a special performance fabric upholstery that resists fading and is forgiving of spills.

Unfortunately, however, the textile is only partly pet-proof: the bouclé finish has become the cat's favourite scratching spot in the house. The sofa, as a result, is fraying at the edges. Which begs the question: what would Issoufou replace it with, if she designed it herself? "Something cat-resistant," she says, laughing, noting that in her career, which has kept her busy making buildings, she has never drawn up a sofa. "It's something I would love to do, because somehow they always have great importance in our lives. I see it as one of those pieces of furniture that is not to show but to live with."

35.
Chatpong Chuenrudeemol
On a custom-made sofa

Bangkok, Thailand

Defying easy categorisation, Chatpong Chuenrudeemol's four-metre-long sofa is an efficient, multifunctional hybrid solution to space-starved Southeast Asian living demands. It shows the importance – and quiet power – of furniture that adapts rather than dictates.

Sofa designer
Chatpong Chuenrudeemol

Manufacturer
Custom made

Year designed
2005

About the sofa
Chatpong Chuenrudeemol designed this four-metre-long built-in sofa for his own home in Bangkok. Tucked between two matching side tables (also built-in, with intricately contoured table lamps on top), the sofa lacks formal backrests, with comfort added by pillows that lean directly onto the wall and window frames instead. It's built using humble materials: neem wood (*mai sadao*) for the frame and cladding that has been wire-brushed to accentuate the grain. It's a versatile piece of furniture that is compact in footprint, and an integral part of his daily life.

About the owner
Chatpong Chuenrudeemol is one of Thailand's top contemporary architects. In 2012, he established his Bangkok-based studio Chat Architects, before setting up the Chat Lab research practice in 2015. Between the two, Chuenrudeemol produces architectural and research work that is driven by a deep understanding of vernacular design, inspired by the informal architecture (which he calls "Bangkok bastards") found on his hometown's streets. Portfolio highlights include the Angsila Oyster Scaffolding Pavilion and the Samsen Street Hotel in Bangkok, which blend local construction wisdom with contemporary design.

The sofa at Chatpong Chuenrudeemol's home playfully challenges the traditional notion of what this furniture typology can be. "It's a combination of a sofa and a built-in seat," says the Thai architect of the custom-made piece located beneath a window in his home in Bangkok's Ekkamai neighbourhood. The work is really a melange of furniture solutions: a bench, daybed, storage cabinet, workstation and even a seat for a bay window overlooking a shaded yard. Designed by the architect himself, it's where his family has spent most evenings since the house was built in the 2000s – and that shouldn't come as a surprise, given its multifunctionality. Chuenrudeemol's version of comfort isn't about plush cushions or ergonomic design, but the ability for furniture to adapt to various needs, melding effortlessly into one's life.

"When I was designing my house, I tried to conserve space by building the sofa right into the wall," says Chuenrudeemol. The result is a piece of furniture that defines a space, while also offering various usage options. Chuenrudeemol sits here to work on his laptop, leaning into one of the pillows, feet up. Often, he can also be found sketching on wide sheets of paper pulled over a side table. Any accoutrements the architect wants nearby can be found in the generously proportioned built-in drawers located beneath fabric-covered cushions. "It's almost the scale of a room," he says about the sofa's four-metre length. It also sleeps two people, with Chuenrudeemol referring to it as a "bunk bed" where his son would host sleepovers as a child, adding another usage to the sofa's list of functions.

"I'd rather have one thing that does many things," says Chuenrudeemol. "This approach is really based on this 'Bangkok bastards' ideology I have developed, where I hybridise things that are known. It's something that is kind of hacked and has no proper lineage." Despite its "bastardised" multi-functionality, the sofa is sleek, with its anatomical and functional flexibility not readily obvious. It's a trait that's inherent in much of Chuenrudeemol's research-driven work, which is deeply rooted in his understanding of his hometown's vernacular energy (both polished and gritty – or steamy, even) and the lifestyles of Southeast Asia. "Living in Bangkok, Jakarta, Kuala Lumpur, we will all have to deal with dense populations and space that becomes harder to come by. So we have to be efficient with everything that we do in design," he says. "The sofa epitomises this

"In Thai life, once we have dinner, we retire upstairs – and this is where we retire to. This sofa is a part of our family's history"

idea; it's not just a piece of loose furniture, it's part of the architecture as well, part of the story of this house."

It's a plot that the sofa will continue to contribute to. Sitting in the connecting family room between his and his wife's bedroom and his son's, the built-in sofa is where the family's activity takes place towards the end of the day. "In Thai life, once we have dinner, we retire upstairs – and this is where we retire to," says Chuenrudeemol. "This sofa is a part of our family's history."

36.
David Thulstrup
& Martin Nielsen
On the Karm sofa

Copenhagen, Denmark

After years abroad and with a global portfolio, architect David Thulstrup has returned to his hometown of Copenhagen. Here, in his former family home, two Karm sofas serve as stationary points of calm, responding to the rhythms of daily life, from family gatherings to quiet nights in.

Sofa designer
David Thulstrup

Manufacturer
Brdr Krüger

Year designed
2018

About the sofa
The Karm sofa was designed by David Thulstrup for Noma, embodying the natural elegance of the world-famous Copenhagen restaurant. Its distinctive form features a generous, deep seat and monolithic armrests, providing a welcoming, sculpted presence. Crafted for enduring comfort, the design pairs a solid oak frame with high-density foam and premium upholstery. The Karm sofa reflects Thulstrup's ethos of timelessness, precise detailing, and honest materials, creating a luxurious and quietly assertive centrepiece for any discerning interior.

About the owner
Danish architect David Thulstrup, a graduate of the Royal Danish Academy of Design, honed his skills working for esteemed architects Jean Nouvel in Paris and Peter Marino in New York. He established his own studio in Copenhagen in 2009 and now leads a practice celebrated for the design philosophy that he refers to as "massive materiality". Key projects include the globally acclaimed interior design of Noma restaurant in Copenhagen and Ikoyi restaurant in London, both of which showcase his mastery of atmosphere, as well as numerous elegant residential and commercial projects embodying a contemporary Danish design sensibility.

With a global portfolio of projects including private residences, shops, restaurants and the odd yacht, David Thulstrup is always on the move. But when the architect and designer is in Copenhagen, he loves nothing more than spending time with his husband Martin Nielsen in their apartment.

It's a home that links generations. Thulstrup lived there with his parents when he was a teenager until he graduated from university, whereupon he moved to Paris and then New York. He returned to Copenhagen in 2009 and moved back in as the apartment's primary resident after his father decided to spend more time abroad. "I learned so much when I was away," says Thulstrup, who started his own studio that year too. "But Copenhagen will always be my home." What took place next was a slow and thoughtful process of

"It makes me happy to see the sofas in this home every day. It's a genuine pleasure to have them in our lives"

turning the space into his and Nielsen's long-term residence. "This apartment gave me the perfect opportunity to put down proper roots," says Thulstrup. "It also gives my dad a familiar home from home when he visits."

In 2017 Thulstrup was chosen to design the interiors and furniture for chef René Redzepi's Noma restaurant, changing the trajectory of Thulstrup's career and,

inadvertently, ending his search for the perfect sofa. As part of the project, he designed what is now known as the Karm sofa; its main material is solid oak, retaining the wood's grain and characteristics throughout its entire thickness, and echoing the natural material palette used throughout the restaurant interiors. The oak is expressed in the solid back and arms that wrap around the sofa, enclosing an upholstered seat and cushions. Redzepi was delighted and the Karm sofa went into production with Danish furniture makers Brdr Krüger in 2019. "It was an extraordinary opportunity to create a *Gesamtkunstwerk* – a total design – for Noma," says Thulstrup.

Back at the apartment, in a 19th-century building near Copenhagen's city centre, two three-seater Karms have become central to Thulstrup and Nielsen's life. Their extended family, groups of friends, even clients and business gatherings can easily be accommodated. During the week, the couple like to come home, pour a refreshing drink, grab a blanket and occupy a sofa each to watch TV. "We go all out when we have people over," says Thulstrup. "There will be fresh flowers, laying the table with beautiful plates and glassware we've collected, cooking something special over the course of the day, and making our guests feel happy and content."

Weekends are a little different – the Karms are occupied for reading, chatting, listening to music and generally taking the time to relax and unwind. The result? Two sofas that are a stationary point of calm, containment and comfort in an apartment that has been a focal point of Thulstrup's, his parents' and his siblings' lives – and now his life with Nielsen. "It makes me happy to see the sofas in this home every day," he says. "It's a genuine pleasure to have them in our lives."

37.
Hunn Wai & Olivia Lee
On the Söderhamn sofa

Singapore

The home of Singaporean industrial designers Hunn Wai and Olivia Lee has a tranquil atmosphere. There are no collector pieces or award-winning furniture works from their acclaimed careers on show. Instead, calming cream microcement floors and simple white cabinetry set the tone in their renovated 1970s public housing apartment. "Our day is spent with so much stimulation that we want to come home to a neutral space," says Lee. "We want somewhere we can decompress and recharge by giving our senses a break."

It's an ambition that explains their unassuming sofa choice: Ikea's deep-seated beige Söderhamn. The customised variant has a corner section and is furnished with loose cushions. "The sofa helps to segment our small home," says Lee. "When you walk in, you're greeted by openness, with the sofa separating the bar area from the living room." Its space-shaping qualities also come to the fore in the form of its elevated seat, with the gap between the couch and the floor allowing light to flow beneath the sofa, adding to the overall lightness of the residence.

Positioned at the heart of their home, the sofa bookends the couple's daily routine: they spend their mornings here with a coffee in hand and return at dinner time to watch their favourite TV shows. On weekends, the couch often turns into a daybed for reading or a chaise longue where friends spill out after a drink at their bar. The couple's love for hosting reaffirmed their sofa selection: the Söderhamn's covers are easily washable. Their decision to furnish their home with a sofa that they don't have to be precious about was also informed by visits to friends' homes. On one occasion Wai visited a residence with a white designer settee, but was urged to sit elsewhere in case the dye from his jeans bled onto the fabric. A more welcoming sofa was therefore always part of their plan. "If the door handle is the handshake of a building, the sofa is the hug of your home," says Lee. "It's the thing that will always receive you after a long day."

Sofa designer
Ola Wihlborg

Manufacturer
Ikea

Year designed
2010

About the sofa
Swedish designer Ola Wihlborg created this modular sofa, which allows individual sections to be combined to assemble a custom couch. In keeping with Ikea's flat-pack ethos, the sofa's seat is supported by fabric rather than metal springs, while its cushions are slimmer than those of a typical sofa. Six colours are offered, allowing room for personalisation.

About the owner
Hunn Wai and Olivia Lee are a Singaporean design power couple. Wai is co-founder of Milan and Singapore-based Lanzavecchia + Wai, while Lee leads her namesake studio. Their shared home life no doubt influences their respective work, with common threads in projects for clients including Herman Miller and Hermès (Wai), and Cartier and Vacheron Constantin (Lee). Both have portfolios that not only enhance the human experience but also exude a sense of play and wonder.

38.
David Welsh &
Chris Major
On the 801
Series sofa

Sydney, Australia

For years, the hearth was the heart of the home. Now, according to David Welsh and Chris Major, it's the sofa. A vintage Charles Wilson piece has served their family for more than 20 years, reflecting the potential of an accommodating statement piece to bring people together.

Sofa designer
Charles Wilson

Manufacturer
Woodmark

Year designed
2001

About the sofa
Woodmark began when Danish-born upholsterer Arne Christiansen moved to Australia. Initially he imported designs from Scandinavia before beginning manufacturing with Australian creatives in the 1990s and 2000s, including Sydney-based designer Charles Wilson. Their collaboration yielded hits such as the 801 Series sofa – a handsome and imposing sofa with one foot in the mid-century and the other firmly planted in the optimism of the new millennium. Its minimal profile sympathises with a host of aesthetics, while minor touches such as scalloping, generous cushion surface area and its distinctive metallic sled base give it an identity of its own.

About the owner
Together, David Welsh and Chris Major run a household and a design studio in Sydney. The latter, called Welsh + Major and founded in 2004, is well-regarded for delightful, practical and inspiring architecture that responds to context, history and materiality. Key projects include the transformative Pyrmont Community Centre upgrades, thoughtfully integrating old and new; the adaptively reused Hat Factory in Sydney that celebrates the building's past; and the carefully integrated Seagrass House, a minimalist coastal dwelling designed to fit a unique site.

Partners in business and life, David Welsh and Chris Major's architectural practice emphasises modernity and contextuality. Given that most of the duo's residential and commercial projects take place in Australia, their work is shot through with an indelibly antipodean character. It's the same story at their compact home in Sydney's inner suburbs. Although international design icons are dotted throughout the space, including an original Isamu Noguchi coffee table, they're outnumbered by statement pieces from Down Under. For more than 20 years, a 2.4-metre-long brown leather 801 Series sofa, designed by local industrial designer Charles Wilson for Australian brand Woodmark at the turn of the millennium, has ruled the living-room roost.

But favouring aesthetic patriotism and eschewing the temptation of foreign furniture has yielded practical results for the pair – including a recent re-upholstering. "I emailed Charles the other day, and he came back to me and said, 'Go to this upholsterer, they know my work from that period,'" says Major. "That's not something you can get if you buy your sofa from overseas," says Welsh. "Now it looks beautiful again and there's a nice sustainability story there too."

Other pieces, such as a pair of classic Roger McLay Kone chairs, have come and gone in the living area over the past two decades but none have outlasted the 801 sofa. "It's the hearth of the house, really," says Welsh. "This brown lounger is the thing that everything pivots around." Its placement in the open-plan room is testament to that; visual punctuation that delineates the kitchen and dining space from the living area and provides a demarcation between the indoors and the courtyard. "So it works as an item in the room that you appreciate but it also facilitates how you see the room," says Major. "A lot of the houses we design are delivery systems for living your life, and

this lounger also does that for us in so many respects," adds Welsh.

The 801 is also positioned to take advantage of the living room's three-sided clerestory, which provides welcome natural light in winter, as well as views of the garden's leaves as they change with the seasons. For Welsh, it's been the perfect background for many a nap on the 801. "Watching the world through those windows, particularly when the children were small and you'd be sitting with them on the lounger while they slept or watched TV, are some of my favourite memories," says Major. Every time the

> "A lot of the houses we design are delivery systems for living your life, and this lounger does that for us in so many respects"

idea of replacing the sofa has come up, the notion has been scrapped pretty quickly. "We've contemplated it but we don't know what we'd replace it with," says Welsh. "We'd be very sad to part with it now."

Over the years, the 801 has weathered countless parties, reading marathons, film nights, friends overstaying their welcome and the chaos of bringing up children and dogs. "It's seen many wars, this one," says Major, but despite all of the patina and battle scars, there's only been one consistent rule over the past 20 years: "David's got his side and I've got mine."

39.
Fien Muller & Hannes Van Severen
On the Pillow sofa

Evergem, Belgium

"We like to live with our own pieces," says Fien Muller, one half of Belgian studio Muller Van Severen, which she co-founded with Hannes Van Severen in 2011. "We want to know how they behave in real life." That includes the couch at their home in Evergem, not far from Ghent. Produced by BD Barcelona, it was first shown at Milan's furniture fair Salone del Mobile in 2024; following the event one of the newly displayed Pillow sofas was hoisted onto a truck and transported from the Lombard capital directly up to Belgium. Since then, the mint-green three-seater has served as the couple's family couch.

The Pillow sofa was originally conceived in 2020 as a limited edition for German clothing brand Kassl Editions and was soon put into wider production by BD Barcelona. Significantly, it was the first soft couch designed by Muller Van Severen and required many iterations to get right. "A sofa is a really difficult thing to design," says Muller. "It has to be super comfortable or it doesn't make sense." The pair took inspiration from Kassl Editions' Pillow Bag but it also looks like louche Italian classics from the 1980s, like Mario Bellini's Camaleonda (*see page 207*) and Vico Magistretti's Maralunga (*see pages 10 and 208*). "All our favourites are from this era," says Van Severen.

At home in Evergem, the Pillow sofa's predecessor was an Amanta by Bellini. There are few sofas that would succeed as follow-up acts to an Italian design classic but the Pillow sofa has passed the live-in test with flying colours. With its plush seats and prime placement, the couch has become a favourite lounging spot for both two and four-legged members of the household. "I often fall asleep on it myself," says Van Severen. "I watch TV in the evening and the next thing I know I'm awake in the middle of the night, thinking, 'Where am I?'" On several occasions, the couple has also put up house guests on it for the night. "Nobody has ever complained in the morning," says Van Severen.

Sofa designer
Muller Van Severen

Manufacturer
BD Barcelona

Year designed
2020

About the sofa
Inspired by Kassl Editions' signature line of padded handbags, the Pillow sofa has a deep, slouchy form held together by soft straps. It is produced by Spanish outfit BD Barcelona, has a modular structure and can be upholstered in bright-hued leathers, velvets, corduroys and cottons. By simply untying a strap, the sofa can be taken apart and reassembled into any size and colour combination.

About the owner
Belgian couple Fien Muller and Hannes Van Severen are a design duo known for creating work that blurs the line between art and furniture, employing bold forms, vibrant colours and materials such as steel, brass and marble. Key pieces include the Neon lighting range, characterised by colourful glass neon tubes in exotic draped shapes, and the Wire seats, where wire frames form simple yet highly sculptural seats.

40.
Niall & Helen Maxwell
On the FD147L sofa

Carmarthenshire, Wales, UK

Philosophies can cross borders. Despite being based in Wales, Niall Maxwell feels a connection to Danish mid-century design, where emphasis is placed on craft and quality. It's an outlook that he embeds in his own practice – proving that unique works can be created from universal ideals.

Sofa designer
Hvidt & Mølgaard

Manufacturer
France & Daverkosen

Year designed
1951

About the sofa
The FD147L sofa was designed by Hvidt & Mølgaard – a studio led by Peter Hvidt and Orla Mølgaard-Nielsen – for France & Daverkosen in the 1950s. It is a benchmark for mid-century Danish design's effortless elegance. Its solid teak frame and woven rattan backrest allow light to gracefully pass through the furniture, creating a visually sculptural presence regardless of where it is located. Despite its simplicity, the piece is not short of innovation – its ingenious locking metal connections enable flat-packing for easier transport or storage.

About the owner
Niall Maxwell studied architecture at University College London before moving from the UK capital to rural Wales in the early 2000s with his wife, Helen. By 2008 he had founded his own practice, Rural Office in Carmarthen, championing a design language that reinterprets vernacular traditions. It's a philosophy that produces work that is rooted in place and has a deep respect for the local environment. Portfolio highlights include Caring Wood, a Kent country house with oast-inspired roofs, and the redevelopment of the National Slate Museum in Snowdonia, Wales.

When Niall Maxwell and his wife, Helen, made the move from London to rural Wales in the early 2000s, it was part of a conscious bid to build a life that was closer to nature. An architect and landscape designer respectively, the duo wanted to practise in ways deeply connected to place, identity and traditional materials – an outlook that extends to the selection of furniture for their homes over the years. Certainly, since before their departure from the UK capital, the duo had filled their spaces with furniture that meets this brief.

To start, there were two 1950s Sawbuck chairs by Hans Wegner. "The story of Danish furniture designers is inextricably linked to the craftsmen who made them," says Maxwell, of the appeal. "Materials, aesthetics and technology are as one." These were followed in due course by a pair of oak and woven cane Carl Hansen & Son CH27 easy chairs, also by Hans Wegner. Indeed, such was their commitment to these particular seats that Helen once spotted a pair up for auction at Christie's and ended up outbidding professional dealers.

With the completion of their farmhouse in Wales, the opportunity came to add a sofa to their collection. After living with the Hans Wegner chairs, the duo recognised that mid-century Danish design philosophy aligned with their own. This prompted them to visit Simon Harrison at Danish Homestore in Nottingham to check his stock for pieces that might be suitable for their own residence. "Back when we first started looking, Danish mid-century furniture was relatively affordable," says Maxwell. "Simon would find treasures from vintage sellers back in Denmark and bring them to the UK."

The result of the hunt was an FD147L sofa – an elegant 1950s teak-framed seat with a woven-cane back by Denmark's Peter Hvidt and Orla Mølgaard-Nielsen. Creative partners and founders of their namesake practice, Hvidt & Mølgaard, the two are little known beyond Denmark, where they collaborated from 1944 until both retired in 1975. In their catalogue are works as vast as the Little Belt Bridge, which spans a strait between Jutland and the island of Funen, and chairs such as the Portex from 1945, which established them as designers of note.

The great appeal of the FD147L sofa – and part of the genius of Hvidt & Mølgaard's work – is its ability to feel generously proportioned, while maintaining a visual lightness and an understated presence. "So many contemporary sofas are great lumps of

"So many contemporary sofas are great lumps of upholstery. They take up space and attention and are too bed-adjacent"

upholstery. They take up space and attention and are too bed-adjacent," says Maxwell, adding that the FD147L stands in stark contrast. "I think of it with the same frame of reference as the architecture that it sits in – it is a work of craft, handmade, made from natural materials, timeless and unconnected to fashion or trends." The result is nothing short of an artistic triumph – something that isn't lost on the couple. "The sofa is like a painting – sculptural and architectural. We get as much pleasure from seeing it as we would from looking at a painting on the wall and would never have anything else."

41.
Fernanda Canales
On the Siesta sofa

La Reserva
Peñitas, Mexico

Despite being her own design,
Fernanda Canales says that the
sofa at her weekend house is a
work of non-design. Instead,
the architect's cornerpiece
transforms through the day –
morning yoga mat, afternoon
desk, evening siesta spot and
family games table.

Sofa designer
Fernanda Canales

Manufacturer
Custom-made

Year designed
2019

About the sofa
When Fernanda Canales wanted to create a sofa for her own weekend retreat in Mexico, she knew that it had to reflect the architecture of the residence itself. The Terreno House blends with the surrounding landscape, so it was only fitting that the resulting Siesta sofa did the same indoors. It is positioned against the living room's plywood-panelled walls that fold and slide onto themselves to reveal big panoramic windows, allowing the user to choose whether they want to feel cocooned or make the most of indoor-outdoor configurations.

About the owner
Mexican architect Fernanda Canales is celebrated for her rigorous approach to architecture, often exploring the interplay between public and private space. Her ethos prioritises contextual sensitivity and social engagement – an approach that sees her perfectly placed to create thoughtful works of architecture that enhance daily life, whether for a community-minded project or private residence. Portfolio highlights include the Elena Garro Cultural Centre in Mexico City, a masterful renovation balancing heritage with contemporary needs, and Casa 720, where the structure is seamlessly integrated with the natural surroundings.

"It's based on the idea of a non-design piece of furniture," says Fernanda Canales. The Mexican architect is explaining her design approach to a custom sofa that she created for her weekend house. "It's meant to be an extension of the space, rather than an object," she says, adding that at the outset, all she had in mind was for the bespoke lounge to take up a nook in the corner of the living room. "I don't like the idea that furniture defines the space. It should be the other way around."

It's this thoughtful outlook that led Canales to create a boxy, plywood frame that encloses a large, daybed-like sofa; it is both simple and flexible and is part of a set that includes tables with expandable components and moveable wood elements. "Its size means that you can lie down or sit up. You can sleep, eat, play. Sometimes it works as a table where we play backgammon or work on a laptop," says Canales. "You're allowed to use the extension and are not conditioned by whatever activity it was used for previously. It's funny because every member of the family has their own position linked to it – even the dog."

Canales puts the multifunctionality of her sofa to good use when she's at the home. The day often starts with *pranayama* yoga on the sofa's extended seating, which serves as her yoga mat, before the couch switches functions to serve as a desk as she has calls with clients and with her studio. After lunch it's time for a siesta – the activity that the sofa is named after. And there's always plenty of space for her to play with her kids too. "This sofa, for me, means anonymity," she says. "It allows me to redefine the way I do things. It's anonymous because it really changes throughout the day. I don't need to be sitting down at a desk to do work or sit down in a certain way if I am entertaining guests. This can be inspiring and actually sometimes better ideas come from sitting

in strange positions and reframing your typical surroundings."

The Siesta sofa's influence hasn't been felt only by Canales. The house itself has evolved due to its presence. "The sofa has really colonised the space. Thanks to the corner in which it is tucked, the rest of the living room has changed too," says Canales, adding that the space used to

"Essentially the sofa improved all the pieces around it because everything needed to be more adaptable in this space"

have a heavy, immovable rectangular coffee table that made it hard to host a range of different activities. "So, I changed it. I designed a couple of moveable tables of different heights, where you can open them and slide the wood surfaces towards you. There are also other lighting options that move too – essentially the sofa improved all the pieces around it because everything needed to be more adaptable in this space."

However, if there's one thing that Canales takes away from all of this, it is the power that a simple piece of furniture can have in extending, rather than defining, the use of a space. "It's a reflection of how living and experiencing a space is very different from just designing it in a floor plan," says Canales. "It was a huge lesson and it has made me a better architect."

42.
Sigurd Larsen
On the A Sofa

Berlin, Germany

Danish architect and furniture designer Sigurd Larsen only emigrated a few hundred kilometres when he chose to set up his practice in Berlin. However, his favourite piece of household furniture, A Sofa – which Larsen created for Copenhagen furniture house Formel A – bridges a greater distance.

"We wanted to make a sofa that had the depth and comfort of an Italian sofa but the lightness and elegance of a Scandinavian sofa," says Larsen, adding that the latter tends to be raised on legs. "We Scandinavians have an urge to make things light, to have the light shine through. By contrast, most Italian sofas don't have legs; they're deep and lounge-like – just blocks on the ground."

Larsen successfully brought these distinct qualities together in A Sofa – so much so that he decided to choose one for his own fifth-floor apartment, which he shares with his husband. The duo decided to place the sofa at the heart of the home, landing it in a prime spot near the kitchen. "The kitchen and living room are one continuous space," says Larsen. "So, it's the centrepiece of the apartment."

Though the chimeric, intracontinental quality of A Sofa was clear from the beginning, by living with his own creation Larsen has discovered other qualities in his design. Namely, it's long and deep enough to serve as an additional bed, when Larsen's guest bedroom is occupied. "I'm 190cm tall and tend to design things that are a bit bigger than the standard sizes," he says, laughing.

Importantly, the sofa is also strong enough to withstand hard partying. "We have had so many spontaneous parties, with people dancing on the sofa," he says, explaining that his design can take a knock or two and still look good. "If things break by being used, they aren't good enough," says Larsen. "We've spilled lots of stuff on the sofa and you can clean it with water. I'm not afraid of patina."

Sofa designer
Sigurd Larsen

Manufacturer
Formel A

Year designed
2017

About the sofa
Sigurd Larsen's A Sofa, for Copenhagen furniture house Formel A, places a generously sized, Italianate sofa body on slender, Scandinavian-style legs. Available as a large and small sofa, as well as a club-chair model, the furniture is handcrafted in the EU. The lightness of the legs, which are available in oak or copper, offsets the sumptuousness of the upholstery. Larsen likens it to a room within a room, floating in space.

About the owner
Architect and designer Sigurd Larsen follows in the Danish tradition of working on all aspects of a development, from landscaping and architecture through to the interiors, drawing no strong divide between building and product design. Portfolio highlights include the Løvtag treetop hotel in Denmark, which uses elevated cabins to immerse guests in nature, and his Shrine cabinet, featuring hidden compartments that play with notions of secrecy and discovery.

43.
Tamsin Johnson
On a custom-made sofa

Sydney, Australia

Childhood can have a lasting impact on adult life. For Tamsin Johnson growing up perched on "The Bench" – her friend's nickname for her antique-dealer mother's rock-hard 19th-century French sofa – meant she was determined never to repeat that discomfort.

Sofa designer
Tamsin Johnson

Manufacturer
Custom made

Year designed
2021

About the sofa
Interior designer Tamsin Johnson created her own sofa to the precise specifications of its intended purpose. Situated in her downstairs living area, an indoor-outdoor room that overlooks a pool, the nearly four-metre-long L-shaped sofa is made from textured, tough two-tone biscuit-and-cream-coloured bouclé (resulting in an overall soft peach tone), trimmed extravagantly with white tasselled fringing on the back cushions and skirt. To realise the sofa, she enlisted the talents of one of her long-time contractors, using upholstery provided by C&C Milano.

About the owner
Australian interior designer Tamsin Johnson, who established her practice in 2013, is celebrated for her refined yet relaxed aesthetic that works across residential, hotel and restaurant projects. Based in Sydney and with projects across Australia, as well as in New York, Paris and London, she draws on her upbringing to blend pieces across decades and continents, creating spaces that feel both beautiful and effortlessly liveable.

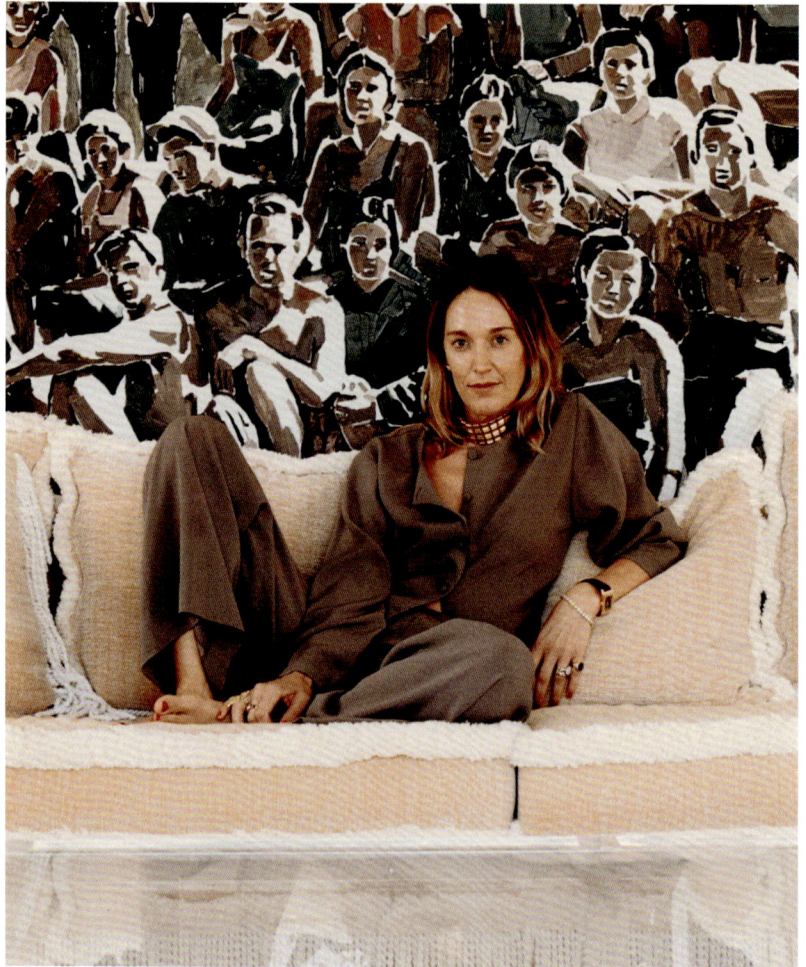

To understand Tamsin Johnson's decision to commission a bespoke sofa for her home, one needs to know that she is the daughter of one of Melbourne's most esteemed antique dealers. As such, she grew up in a house bedecked with curios, chinoiseries, arabesque banquettes – and one very uncomfortable sofa. "My best friend nicknamed it 'The Bench' because it was this rock-hard 19th-century French number in a silk damask with wooden arms that was only about 60 centimetres deep," says Johnson.

Despite the occasional discomfort it engendered, Johnson's upbringing gave her

> "It's still at the beginning of its career but there might need to be some steam cleaning. Sofas can very much be saved and have nine lives"

an immaculate eye that has seen her become one of Australia's most sought-after interior designers. Her interiors have won steady acclaim for the ways in which they seamlessly accommodate both old and new.

It's the same story at the harbourside home in Sydney that she shares with her husband, fashion designer Patrick Johnson, and their two children. The house's antique furnishings don't genuflect at the altar of their own age. Instead, Johnson has assimilated them into the bright – and comparatively contemporary – space. It's an environment that gives the interiors a shot of timeworn gravitas, while affording the vintage pieces a new lease on life. "Being an antique dealer, as well as an interior designer, my spaces are quite naturally layered with antiques," says Johnson. "So, I wanted the sofa to be more subtle and work more as a backdrop, rather than competing with the rest."

Johnson could have dipped into her antique dealership for a subtle sofa or leveraged her brand knowledge to identify the perfect newer model. But instead, she decided to design her own. And she knew exactly what she didn't want. "The first thing I thought about was comfort," says Johnson. "It is key – I'm not having another bench."

While custom sofas don't boast the same romantic backstories as their vintage counterparts, they more than make up for this by being uniquely suited to the spaces – and functions – that they occupy. For the Johnsons' downstairs sofa, which overlooks the pool, a comfortable fabric that provided resilience was the highest priority. "It's very much an indoor-outdoor room," says Johnson. "So, it's a glamorous-looking sofa but it needs to be grounded in the practical realities of the pool and the kids." It's a large, fringed piece, with two kinds of trim, upholstered in a tough yellowy-taupe bouclé. "The downstairs sofa is very mixed-purpose," says Johnson. "I'm obsessed with using outdoor fabrics in people's homes because, as boring as it sounds, practical sofas are that important."

The sofa has had to be adaptable, playing host to everything from children's sleepovers to the occasional nap during the summer cricket. "A sofa to me isn't the main character of a room but it's still the backbone of the space." Though the children's regular jousts with the sofa are ageing it, its tenacity is a big part of its charm. "It's still at the beginning of its career but there might need to be some steam cleaning," says Johnson. "Sofas can very much be saved and have nine lives."

44.
Dorte Mandrup
On the Poet sofa

Copenhagen,
Denmark

Long aware of a sofa's ability to dictate the feel of a room, architect Dorte Mandrup finally embraced Finn Juhl's iconic Poet sofa. The mid-century masterpiece breaks from the mould of much Danish furniture, with its whimsical form providing the perfect relaxing nook.

Sofa designer
Finn Juhl

Manufacturer
House of Finn Juhl

Year designed
1941

About the sofa
Danish mid-century architect Finn Juhl designed the Poet sofa in 1941 for his own home in Ordrup, north of Copenhagen. The compact two-seater reflects Juhl's pioneering approach to design, combining comfort with sculptural form. Now produced by House of Finn Juhl – the only company licensed to manufacture his designs – the sofa is handmade by skilled craftsmen. Inspired by surrealist art, the sofa's rounded silhouette creates a sense of intimacy – ideal for reading, quiet conversation or lounging.

About the owner
Copenhagen-based Dorte Mandrup studied medicine and sculpture before finding her métier in architecture. Mandrup's designs are both fearless and meticulous, often tackling complex cultural and environmental challenges. Growing up in North Zealand in the northeast of Denmark, she developed a sensitivity to landscapes, which shapes the work of her namesake practice today. An example is the Ilulissat Icefjord Centre in Greenland, an award-winning project that is a reflection on ice, climate and heritage, blending bold design with conservation.

For years, Dorte Mandrup didn't own a sofa. "It's one of those pieces of furniture that determines so much of the space," says the Danish architect from the top floor of her two-storey Copenhagen apartment. "They're often large and take up a lot of room so you want to think carefully about the one you bring into your home."

She had, however, long set her sights on a favourite design: the Poet sofa by Finn Juhl. The mid-century Danish architect originally created it for his own home and presented it for the first time in 1941 at Copenhagen's Cabinetmakers' Guild, the annual furniture fair at the time in Denmark. Its design features soft, organic curves with distinct, spiking edges – a nod to Juhl's fascination with surrealist art.

The moment that Mandrup saw one of these iconic mid-century sofas up for auction, she seized the opportunity and brought home the two-seater, upholstered in light-green fabric. "I love it," she says. "It's small enough not to take up the whole room but big enough to lounge on."

Mandrup placed Juhl's design on the lower floor of her home – part of a residential building tucked away on a quiet street in the city's lively Nørrebro district, which she and her husband completed in 2022. The sofa sits beneath a thick wooden beam, an architectural detail present in both her home and studio. "It's a cosy spot, perfect for everyday things like reading or just checking your emails," she says.

But it wasn't just the sofa's practicality that drew her in. It's the symbolism behind its design that Mandrup finds compelling. "Juhl was a revolutionary," she says, noting how the shape of the sofa was radically unconventional for its time, featuring whimsical forms in an era mostly defined by strict, geometric lines. "That kind of freedom he took, to think independently and go his own

way, is incredible," she says, adding that his work, so celebrated today, was often criticised by his peers. "That conviction he had to push his own designs forward, no matter how the surroundings were reacting – well, it paid off."

It's a spirit Mandrup brings to her own work. She founded her practice in 1999 with a focus on inventive projects that celebrate the character of each site. A fine example is the Wadden Sea Centre in western Jutland – a large visitor centre and exhibition space in Denmark's biggest national park that revived the region's traditional reed thatching

"The Poet sofa is small enough not to take up the whole room but big enough to lounge on"

techniques. She also shares her experience as a design critic at Harvard University. "I encourage my students to always go their own way," she says. "If you simply do what's in fashion, you're already behind."

Now that the sofa is in place (her daughter had long advocated for getting a sofa, saying a home feels "unfriendly" without one), Mandrup might be considering one final addition to bring a little extra company into the apartment: when the time is right she would love to welcome a cat into her home. And would the pet be allowed to share the couch with her? Mandrup doesn't hesitate: "For sure."

45.
Joyce Wang
On a custom-made sofa

Hong Kong, China

When Joyce Wang sought a new space for her Hong Kong studio, she wanted every element custom-made – especially the sofas. For years her in-studio couch had caused back pain and she was determined to replace it with a sofa that was comfortable, as well as stylish enough to impress guests and clients. "Sofas tend to be statement pieces in and of themselves," says Wang.

Working with Hong Kong craftsman Jackson Law, the interior designer created an olive-green mohair corner sofa after going through months of trial and error to perfect the cushions, fabric and seams. Production took two months, with the sofa manufactured in Law's factory in China. The fabric was stitched so that the seams appear invisible and the cushions were filled out as much as possible to avoid gaps between seats. Discreet charging ports were added to the base of the sofa upon installation. "As you come into the foyer of the studio, you see it – it's kind of a nook at the end of the space," she says. "It's a standalone piece."

The location of the sofa means that for anyone walking in for the first time, it forms a central part of their initial impression. Wang says that she was quick to choose green as its colour; she wanted something that alluded to Hong Kong's abundant nature and greenery, especially as the studio is in the city centre.

Wang calls the sofa's domain "the coffee corner" as it's where she often holds informal meetings or invites friends for a chat over a cappuccino. The right-angle shape allows those seated on it to almost face each other, while its relatively compact size – it can seat "four people at a squeeze" – lends it a comfortable intimacy. "I feel like conversations happen better when you're tucked in a corner," says Wang. "People come and say, 'Oh, this feels like home.'" That sense of home extends into the collective attitude towards the sofa. Colleagues eat lunch there, Wang's children jump around on it during their visits and even the occasional office dog is permitted in the vicinity. "It's very multiuse," says Wang.

Sofa designer
Joyce Wang

Manufacturer
Jackson Law

Year designed
2024

About the sofa
Joyce Wang enlisted furniture-maker Jackson Law to create a bespoke four-seater corner sofa. She made an initial sketch, then Wang and Law spent four months perfecting the details, after which the sofa was manufactured in Law's factory in China. A mixture of feather and synthetic polyfill was used for the stuffing to achieve firm support and the fabric is stitched so that the seams disappear.

About the owner
Joyce Wang is the founder and principal of her namesake interior-design practice, based in Hong Kong and London. Born in Hawaii, raised in Hong Kong and educated at MIT in the US and at the RCA in London, her work reflects her passion for a broad range of cultural influences. Her portfolio includes restaurants – such as The Magistracy and Mott 32 in Hong Kong – and hotels, including London's Mandarin Oriental Hyde Park and The Hollywood Roosevelt in Los Angeles.

46.
Federica Biasi &
Moreno Vannini
On the Niveaux sofa

Milan, Italy

Federica Biasi's signal that work is over comes not from clocking out, but from connecting with her sofa. The grey Niveaux that anchors her Milan apartment was designed with her own comfort in mind and serves as a daily retreat and evening cinema seat for classic films.

Sofa designer
Federica Biasi

Manufacturer
Lema

Year designed
2022

About the sofa
Niveaux takes its name from the French word for "levels" and is a large, beautifully conceived and constructed modular floor sofa, which can be reconfigured in a number of different ways to accommodate different modes of living. The seating bases are square, rectangular and asymmetrical, and are complemented by side tables and a series of moveable cushions and backrests. Less a self-contained sofa and more a reconfigurable seating system, Niveaux hides its unconventional qualities behind fine detailing and stitching, as well as muted, *ton-sur-ton* colourways.

About the owner
Federica Biasi is a Milan-based designer and art director celebrated for her refined aesthetic and focus on tactile beauty. Her studio, established in 2015, blends Nordic influences, Dutch precision (influenced by her time in the Netherlands), Italian craftsmanship and an appreciation for manual work and traditions across product design, furniture and lighting, with clients ranging from boutique brands to global industrial design behemoths.

Federica Biasi is no slouch. The multi-award-winning Italian designer has produced acclaimed work for renowned furniture companies such as Gervasoni, Lema and Emu, as well as brands that are household names such as Nespresso. However, when she steps through the door of her residence on a work-day evening and lays eyes on one particular creation, she knows that it's time to relax. "I enter my home, see my sofa and say, 'OK, the day is done,'" she says. "It's the first place I go."

The welcoming perch in question is the Niveaux model that Biasi created for the Italian brand Lema in 2022. It's a large,

"We'll have to wait for something super-technological to arrive to change the sofa"

low, modular and relatively uncomplicated piece of furniture, which can be rearranged, divided and reconfigured. The Milan-based creative says that it was designed with her own house and tastes in mind. "I'm not looking for something eccentric or crazy but something comfy for me," says Biasi, adding that despite its understated nature, the sofa is rich in smaller details, such as piping around the upholstery. "It's super simple but with a bit of character."

The apartment that she shares with her partner, product designer Moreno Vannini, is more or less decorated in a single shade of grey and the sofa matches this colourway. "It's a super-relaxing monotone house," says Biasi. Her sofa lies in the middle of this home, between the entrance and the kitchen, and is where the couple spend a great deal of time, sitting together, eating and watching classic movies and world cinema (most evenings they'll watch a film). There are no formal rules regarding the sofa. Biasi says that Vannini is super tidy and would like to prohibit food from being eaten on the sofa. "But it doesn't work like that," she says, laughing. Were she to pick another sofa, Biasi says that she would find the choice tough but she would probably go for another low, Italian classic from an earlier era: the Camaleonda sofa designed in 1970 by Mario Bellini is a favourite and a source of inspiration.

Despite her success with the Niveaux, Biasi says that the process of designing a sofa is uniquely challenging. "It's one of the most difficult commissions," she explains. "It's hard to make a good, new sofa and find the right company to develop it. But when it's well done, it's one of the best objects to design in a house; it's the king of the house." Despite this challenge, Biasi is hopeful that new innovations, such as artificial intelligence and other digital, interactive features will lead to wider disruptions in the soft furnishings sector. "We'll have to wait for something super-technological to arrive to change the sofa," she says. Until that time, Biasi is quite happy to spend her evenings ensconced on her low-tech, simple, comfy, characterful model – a labour of love of which she says, "When I see it, I feel warm and relaxed."

47.
Ronan Bouroullec
On the Slow sofa

Paris, France

According to Ronan Bouroullec, a well-designed object should subtly direct the atmosphere of a room. For proof, look to his Slow sofa. Its compact form shows that rather than being a heavy, immoveable focal point, sofas can be a gossamer addition that brings light and levity.

Sofa designer
Ronan &
Erwan Bouroullec

Manufacturer
Vitra

Year designed
2025

About the sofa
Part of Ronan & Erwan Bouroullec's Slow collection, produced by Swiss furniture firm Vitra, this sofa stands as a testament to their innovative material approach. First launched in 2006 with the Slow chair, this collection ingeniously employs a highly engineered knitted fabric, precisely stretched over a minimalist tubular steel frame. The Slow sofa, launched in 2025, is an evolution of the line with a new, more environmentally responsible textile that functions as a comfortable supportive sling.

About the owner
Growing up, Paris-based Ronan Bouroullec found freedom in nature and constraint in the family workshop. Working with his brother Erwan, he has transformed those dual influences into a design philosophy rooted in modularity and adaptability. Beyond his iconic furniture lines for the likes of Vitra and Ligne Roset, Bouroullec's boundary-pushing practice extends to art too. The immersive *Textile Field* installation at London's V&A and his colourful bas-reliefs exemplify his fluid approach to his practice more broadly, bridging functional design with pure artistic expression.

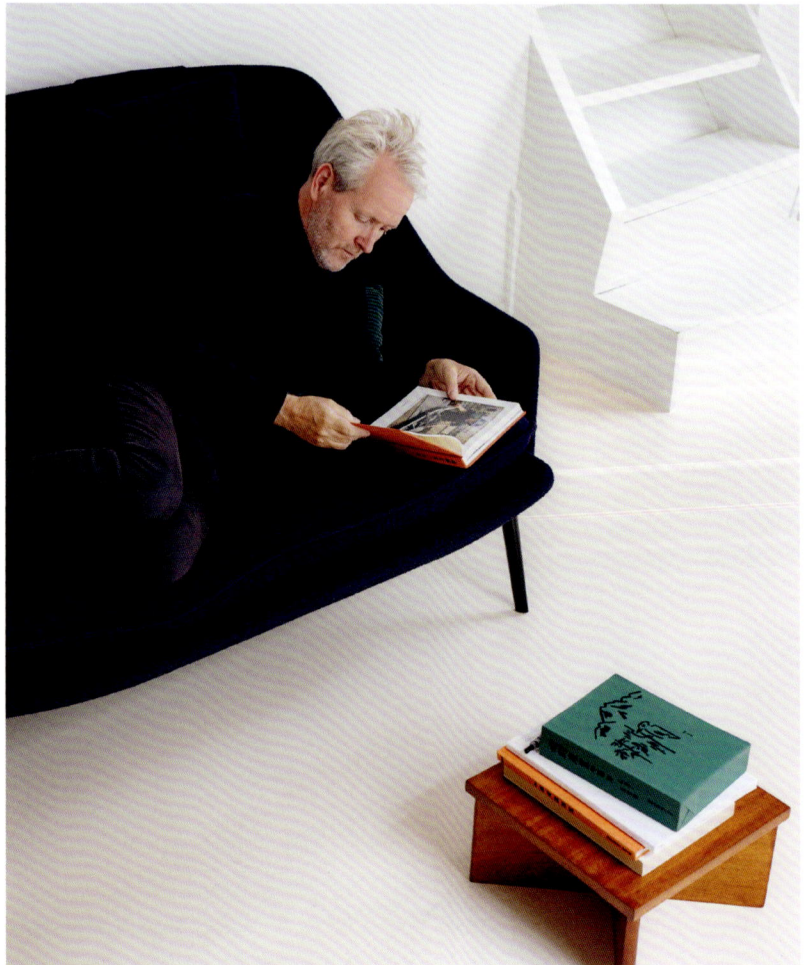

When asked what makes a good design object, Ronan Bouroullec likes to use the image of a teabag steeping in a glass of hot water. "Like a teabag infusing its taste and colour, such an object can change the mood – not only of a space but also of the person using it," says the French industrial designer, who made a name for himself with the furniture he dreamed up alongside his brother,

"This sofa is perfect for curling up in with a book or taking a nap with your child – it's like a basket that envelops you"

Erwan. "It should be something that immediately makes you feel good."

Though he's speaking broadly about design, he may well be referring to the Slow sofa, located in his atelier in Paris's 10th arrondissement. Debuted at the 2025 edition of Copenhagen creative festival 3 Days of Design, the two-seater is a reinvention of the Slow armchair that the Bouroullec brothers first released with Swiss furniture firm Vitra in 2006. Like the original, the sofa is a delicate balance between lightness and comfort, achieved through its fabric-covered tubular frame, high back and thin cushions. "The whole Slow line is made with very little material to make it more recycling-friendly; the challenge was ensuring the items remained comfortable to sit on," says Bouroullec. "Usually, the more filling and cushions you

have, the cosier it gets. But I can assure you, this sofa is perfect for curling up in with a book or taking a nap with your child – it's like a basket that envelops you." For now, the Slow sofa is where he retreats when he needs a break at the studio but he plans to get one for his home as well. "I like to spend time on a sofa," he adds. "Thinking, drawing, checking emails."

Another feature that Bouroullec appreciates is the model's portability. Because of its light structure, it can easily be moved – whether to chase a ray of morning sun or to rearrange the room layout. "More often than not, the sofa seems fixed within the architecture of a place; you put it in one spot and never move it again," he says. "You forget that in French, furniture is called *mobilier* – as the word implies, something that should be mobile."

Being a two-seater results in a smaller format than your average sofa, making the Slow particularly attractive for urban dwellers. Beyond reducing the environmental footprint, its compact size also addresses another contemporary issue: the need for well-designed pieces that suit even the most limited living spaces. "It has beautiful geometric proportions, which make it pleasant to look at from all angles – even from the back – so it doesn't need to be placed against a wall," says Bouroullec. "It's a designer's job to find solutions to the themes of their day."

Almost 20 years might seem like a long time to create a two-seater version of an armchair but, according to Bouroullec, it was the necessary time to get it right. The key was replacing the original 3D-knitted transparent jersey fabric of the Slow armchair with a thicker alternative for greater mechanical resistance. Will there be a three-seater one day? "That would be nice," says Bouroullec. "But I think it would be a stretch."

48.
Alfredo Paredes
On the Santana sofa

New York, USA

Contemporary takes on
century-old design styles can be
risky – not so for Alfredo Paredes.
His own sofa, dubbed Santana,
draws inspiration from 1920s
Hollywood glamour, combined
with traditional English style. The
result is a seat that offers the best
of both worlds.

Sofa designer
Alfredo Paredes

Manufacturer
Alfredo Paredes Studio

Year designed
2021

About the sofa

Alfredo Paredes' Santana sofa embodies the New York-based designer's signature relaxed luxury. Its generous, low-slung form – defined by a deep seat and ample armrests – is both inviting and sophisticated. The meticulously crafted construction features a wooden frame and eight-way hand-tied springs, ensuring enduring comfort. Furnished with plush, down-wrapped cushions, the Santana offers a deep, sink-in feel that marries classic proportions with contemporary comfort. It's a timeless piece designed for elevated lounging.

About the owner

Alfredo Paredes was educated at the Art Institute of Atlanta and honed his distinctive design style over 33 years at Ralph Lauren, rising to chief creative officer and shaping the brand's iconic lifestyle range. In 2019, he launched Alfredo Paredes Studio, bringing his refined vision to interiors, furniture and product design. His work blends classical influences with easygoing opulence, consistently crafting environments and pieces that exude understated sophistication and timeless comfort.

"Buying a sofa is a commitment," says Alfredo Paredes. "Getting it home or moving it from house to house is a challenge – it's not like buying a car." The New York-based designer, having spent several decades designing furniture for the interiors division of Ralph Lauren and then for his own brand, knows that both clients and homeowners take buying this particular piece of furniture very seriously. He has, over the course of his career, consciously interrogated what it is to design a quality sofa. "Two of the most important elements are depth and comfort," says Paredes. "I like a sofa that you can lounge on, and that you can pile a lot of pillows on. Something that envelops you and that you can curl up on." Indeed, his own sofa – a near three-metre-long Santana couch, which he created for his own label in 2021 – fits such a brief perfectly.

Inspired by the gigantic sofas found at the Chateau Marmont hotel in Los Angeles in the 1920s and 1930s, Paredes created this piece as a nod to old Hollywood glamour. "I reinterpreted it," he says. "It looks more like an English country-house sofa but it has a definite Hollywood vibe." The couch, which takes centre stage in his living room, is upholstered in an oatmeal linen with fringing at the bottom. For added comfort, ample cushions have been piled on and a coyote throw blanket strewn across it. "The sofa has a very calming, luxurious effect on the space," says Paredes, who uses it for hosting and also for moments of solace, mirroring the dual function of his living room, which is for both entertaining and unwinding at the weekend. "You can find me sleeping on this gigantic couch on any quiet Sunday. It's in a very peaceful, hidden-away room."

Thanks to the cosy fireplace, it's also the perfect gathering space during the holidays. Paredes has hosted his pyjama-clad siblings and their children on Christmas mornings. "That is nice," he says, explaining that children and dogs aren't typically allowed on the Santana. But Paredes sometimes makes exceptions over the festive period for parties, and also for his own pooch, Poppy, who is on occasion permitted to climb up on it (indeed, she was granted permission for this book). "If they screw it up, they screw it up," says Paredes, laughing. "But I try not to make a big deal about it."

"Buying a sofa is a commitment: getting it home or moving it from house to house is a challenge"

As someone who has designed many sofas before, including more than 10 for his own label, one of the greatest challenges for Paredes when making a new one is creating something that's both different and timeless. "You're not reinventing the wheel so how do you make it feel relevant, luxurious and something someone will want to have forever? It's about designing something that has longevity," he says. When pushed on exactly what this means, the interior specialist says that form and a willingness to make a statement are really the essential building blocks for any good sofa, as longevity can almost always be ensured through judicious refinishing.

"If you love the shape, you can completely reinvent it a million times over through reupholstery. So if a sofa is good, it's just very glamorous – it can make any room."

49.
Grant Wilkinson & Teresa Rivera
On the Peonia sofa

London, UK

Grant Wilkinson and Teresa Rivera opened their namesake design studio in 2020, the year that their son was born. So it's only natural that the dynamics of a young family would influence their work. "We bake purpose into our designs," says Rivera, sitting in their London home on a mohair-cord sofa that they designed. "When you have a child running around, the reality is that whatever you make has to be both sturdy and scrubbable."

At home, the duo balances the high energy levels associated with a young family through calming interior design: evenly coloured walls and an array of wood-toned furniture – much of it also their own work – with art and family photographs adorning surfaces. "It's nonsensical to us to have something in the house that you don't use. Function should still be the primary consideration," explains Rivera. Their sofa, a three-seater dubbed Peonia, was created for London-based retailer and designer SCP. "We never want to sacrifice on aesthetic," adds Wilkinson, referencing the light tone of their sofa. "It's a battle – we couldn't resist the hue of a beautiful, muted olive fabric."

The sofa, launched in 2023, shares a similar wavy aesthetic to many of the pieces in the Wilkinson & Rivera portfolio. The Peonia, with its seamless base and cinched, curving armrests, has a sense of movement embedded in its form. "We're definitely not square-edged folk," says Wilkinson. "We're obsessed with negative space and how it's activated, much the same way that people look at lighting as being sculptural."

When they aren't building furniture out of their studio in a repurposed Victorian-era railway arch in Camden, the couple can be found at home on the Peonia. And they are more than content with the real estate of their sofa space being encroached upon by a preschooler. "We're real have-dinner-on-the-sofa people," says Wilkinson. "It's partly why we made the Peonia so deep, so that we can all fit comfortably. This is a sofa for families."

Sofa designer
Wilkinson & Rivera

Manufacturer
SCP

Year designed
2023

About the sofa
The design of the Peonia sofa is inspired by the geometry of flower petals, particularly the peony, from which it derives its name. The sofa launched in 2023 as part of SCP's natural and sustainable upholstery collection. Manufactured at the brand's Norfolk factory with a frame made from beech and softwood ply, its low-lying form is defined by its curved backrest and outwardly bowing arms that provide both support and character.

About the owners
Wilkinson & Rivera is a London-based design and manufacturing studio with roots in the UK and the US, founded in 2020 by Grant Wilkinson and Teresa Rivera. Educated in London and Philadelphia respectively, their work reinterprets classic forms with a contemporary, often sculptural, twist. The studio works with British artisans, emphasising slow manufacturing processes, materiality and craftsmanship.

50.
Alex Mustonen
& Anita Maritz
On the Sunday sofa

Catskills,
New York State,
USA

Alex Mustonen renovated his family's Catskills retreat around this Blu Dot sofa. It survived two years of works by migrating from room to room. Now anchored in the sunroom, the sofa serves triple duty – climbing frame for his son, reading nook for himself and instant guest bed.

Sofa designer
Blu Dot

Manufacturer
Blu Dot

Year designed
2018

About the sofa
Minnesota-based furniture firm Blu Dot's Sunday sofa is, as the name suggests, perfect for lounging on at the weekend. It is generously proportioned, with an extra-deep seat and low-slung profile. Its cushions are constructed with high-resiliency foam encased in a feather and down wrap, ensuring a soft seat without letting its user sink too deeply into the couch. The sofa's structural integrity is provided by a kiln-dried American hardwood frame, reinforced with doweled and corner-blocked joinery.

About the owner
Architect Alex Mustonen is co-founder of Snarkitecture, a New York-based collaborative practice that blurs the lines between art and architecture. The firm is known for transforming everyday objects and spaces into unexpected, immersive experiences. Key projects include *The Beach* (a moving installation featuring a pit of one million recyclable, translucent plastic balls), furniture for Finnish company Made by Choice, and their work with brands like Kith and Calvin Klein, where they have reimagined retail environments with distinctive, often monochromatic designs.

Alex Mustonen has taken a less-travelled professional path than most architecture graduates. He co-founded his design practice Snarkitecture in 2008 with artist Daniel Arsham, who he met while they were both studying at The Cooper Union in Manhattan. "Our practice is not art and not architecture," says Mustonen of their output, which spans furniture to public art and interiors. The studio's work, as a result, is not always easily characterised – but it is constantly imbued with a sense of playfulness.

The trained architect, who grew up in Connecticut, moved to New York City in

"It's not an heirloom piece but I love it for what it is: a really good all-round versatile family sofa"

2000 and lived in the same rented apartment for 23 years. During those decades, a few sofas came and went but then in 2017, he and his wife Anita Maritz bought a weekend getaway in the Catskills. "It fulfilled a long-standing dream of mine," says Mustonen. "I wanted to be able to spend weekdays in the city and weekends in the forest where I love making things with my hands and being outside." The house was completely empty when they bought it and a couch was high on the list of priorities. As such, one of the first pieces of furniture purchased was a Sunday sofa from American firm Blu Dot.

"Even though some might think of it as a generic contemporary sofa, it has been a constant and reliable presence in our lives," says Mustonen. "Aside from the comfort it brings, it has remarkably survived years of renovations, during which we just moved it from room to room or worked around it."

Post-renovations, the sofa has now found a permanent space in the sunroom, which also doubles as Mustonen's son's playroom. It fits perfectly at one end of the space but that's not just a fortunate stroke of serendipity. "I purposely made sure that the sofa would fit when I planned the renovation," says Mustonen, explaining that it is positioned as a visual anchor at one end of the room in a spot where it is bathed in natural light. "My son uses it as a climbing frame, I use it to read and slouch around on, and guests use it to sleep – you just take the arms and back cushions off and it's ready to go as a guest bed."

It's a hardworking piece of furniture that clearly earns its keep, with Mustonen confirming its robust nature and explaining that there are few rules for its usage. "We don't let our son paint on it or use markers but other than that, pretty much anything goes," says Mustonen. "The fact that we've practically built a house around it proves it's hardier than your average sofa."

And if hardiness, comfiness and other day-to-day practicalities could be dispensed with, what sofa would he design for himself? "I'd design a sofa made up of a load of pillows that can be repurposed to create whatever kind of sofa out of them that you felt like on the day," says Mustonen. "I imagine it as being like a soft city – a sofa architecture. And I love the idea of a sofa you could have a lot of fun with."

Chapter 02.

Designers on Sofas

The history of the sofa

The sofa: a brief history
Stella Roos

The oldest existing sofa – that is, an upholstered seat with space for several people – is encased in plexiglass at Knole House, a historic country house in Kent, England. The design is a little stiff for modern tastes, with its upright backrest and ornamentation of brass studs, gold and silver thread fringes, and a single tasselled pillow. The two-person couch features an ingenious adjustable design, with sides that can be lowered using strings to look like wide armrests for relaxed situations, or pulled up to be as tall as the backrest for more formal occasions. The upholstery is threadbare but considering it is almost 400 years old, it has survived astonishingly well. England's National Trust, which put up the protective case, considers the seat its "most famous single piece of furniture".

Made in London in about 1635 and called the Knole Settee, it is not technically a sofa: that word only entered the English language, as "saffaw" in about 1700. Part of a 17-piece seating arrangement presumably made for a royal residence, this throne-like seat was made only wide enough to accommodate a monarch and consort sitting side by side. It was acquired by the Sackville family, who owned Knole House in the 17th century, and was used to furnish this grand country estate. Virginia Woolf later used the residence as inspiration for the setting of her novel *Orlando*, about a nobleman who changes gender. When Orlando arrives home as a woman, she lies down on the couch, reflecting that she is finally free from "martial ambition, the love of power" and can enjoy the raptures of "contemplation, solitude, love". The Knole Settee didn't just anticipate the modern shape of the sofa, but came with its attendant cultural, class and literary connotations too.

The idea of the sofa – both as an object and as a space for communal lounging – had arrived in Europe via Turkey from the Arab world. In *One Thousand and One Nights*, a collection of ancient folktales, the character of Scheherazade, a legendary queen, avoids death by sitting the murderous sultan down on a divan (a long, low sofa without a back or arms) and telling him stories night after night. The word "sofa" comes from the Arabic *suffah*, meaning bench, and one of its early definitions in the *Dictionarium Britannicum* is "a sort of alcove much used in Asia furnished with rich carpets and cushions". The word divan is also adopted directly from Turkish, where it refers to a low raised seat in an alcove or against a wall, which is often used for official meetings. To this day, the culture of socialising on sofas is strongest in the Middle East. A *majlis* is a cushioned, carpet-strewn sitting room designated as a place for conversation, which remains a feature of everyday life in much of the Arabic-speaking world.

The earliest known architectural example of lounge seating also comes from Turkey. In Çatalhöyük in southern Anatolia, archaeologists have excavated one of the first human settlements dating back to about 7,000 BCE. The inhabitants of this village had yet to invent doors – residents moved from roof to roof and entered their homes with ladders from above – but their homes did have built-in plaster benches, decorated with horns of wild bulls that were used as fairly imposing armrests. The animal bones are believed to be hunting trophies, which became increasingly precious as the nomadic, hunter-gatherer way of life declined in favour of agrarian and sedentary lifestyles.

Many early conceptions of the sofa were located in semi-public spaces, often outdoors and specifically intended as communal spaces. There are the *majlis* (sitting rooms) in Bedouin tents, or the set-ups of daybeds under pergolas called *cameraria* that Romans used for eating, sleeping and general carousing. Even the Japanese – who have never really warmed up to the concept of sedentary furniture, being satisfied with their tatami mats – have their closest equivalent to the sofa in traditional gardens. At the Katsura Imperial Villa in Kyoto, the emperor and empress sat on low, backless benches. But guests waiting to begin a tea ceremony in the garden were directed to wait on the *sotokoshikake*, a long bench with a backrest and armrests under a thatched canopy.

In many cases, the sofa even preceded the bedroom. The word couch comes from *coucher*, French for "to sleep", suggesting a blurred line between the sofa and the bed. Romans didn't have a dedicated room for sleeping at all, instead retreating to a cupboard-like *cubiculum* if they desired more privacy than was on offer under the pergola.

In late 19th-century Budapest, it was habitual to convert the sofas in the salon into beds at night. Around the same time, the first convertible beds were developed in the United States: an early patent was from an African-American woman named Sarah E Goode in 1885, who invented a wooden cupboard that could be folded out to reveal a mattress. It quickly became clear that starting with a sofa was more practical.

In hard-up agrarian Europe, every piece of furniture in the house had to be multi-functional. One predecessor to the sofa was the wooden chest that could be used for both storage and seating. In Italy, a common traditional wedding gift was the *cassone*, a large, ornamented chest filled with essentials for the newlyweds. The chest itself served as furniture for the new home and was often equipped with armrests, backrests and eventually cushions, becoming an early bench-chest-couch hybrid.

A real, upholstered sofa was long a luxury reserved for upper-class homes. By the time the Knole Settee was manufactured in London, furniture-filled drawing rooms were in vogue among the aristocracy of France and Italy, who financed a flurry of couch innovation. France in the 1700s was one of the most inventive periods in the history of the sofa: this is when craftsmen invented the *canapé*, an upright two- or three-seater; the chaise longue with infinite variations; the *caseuse*, a loveseat that two people could squeeze into; and the *tête-a-tête*, an S-shaped seat that two people could murmur across.

According to Joan DeJean, the author of *The Age of Comfort: When Paris Discovered Casual – and the Modern Home Began*, this period also gave rise to a so-called "sofa attitude", where women and men felt liberated to relax their posture, throw their arm across the backrest, stretch out and be generally louche. One fashion icon of the 18th century, Juliette Récamier, posed in slinky white dresses for so many portraits on a type of gondola daybed (inspired by Venetian boats) that the model is still known by her last name in France. Moral panic ensued. A 1742 novel titled *Le Sopha* satirised the newly horizontal lifestyle of the leisured, libertine classes in a kind of sequel to *One Thousand and One Nights* (the author, Claude Prosper Jolyot de Crébillon, was sent into exile from Paris). The reason that the world's oldest sofa is located in England is that the originals were all thrown into the pyre during the French Revolution.

The English industrialised sofa production, inventing the coiled spring and making mass-produced models common in upper-middle-class drawing rooms. Today, many sofa models are still named after the English cabinetmakers who made them, including the rococo Chippendales, or the aristocrats who commissioned them, such as the stodgy Chesterfield sofa with coiled armrests and tufted upholstery. Starting in the Victorian era, the Knole Settee was endlessly copied and its name has come to refer to any sofa with sides that are as high as the backrest.

The most famous couch of the 19th century also hails from England. Around 1890, Sigmund Freud was given a Victorian daybed by a thankful early patient, Madame Benvenisti. While Freud was developing the techniques of psychoanalysis, he also experimented with the positioning of the couch in his office, eventually settling on having the patient lying down with the feet pointing away from him. Even though the daybed is no longer a staple of psychiatrists' offices, the term "on the therapist's couch" lives on as a universal expression.

Psychological, luxurious, erotic and morally questionable – by the turn of the 20th century, the sofa came loaded with symbolic baggage for a designer to unpack. Yet the sofa initially played only a small supporting role in the arrival of modernism. The modern movement was focused on simplifying the home, taking out the heavy, old furniture of centuries past. In the 1920s, Bauhaus came up with the Frankfurt Kitchen, an efficient model for a mass-produced kitchen, but there was no corresponding Frankfurt Living Room. Its connotations with leisure and idleness also didn't play well with the idea of the home as a "machine for living" espoused by Swiss-French architect Le Corbusier, a leading modernist.

The glory lay in reinventing the chair, and many early modernist sofas are in fact

"Psychological, luxurious, erotic and morally questionable – by the turn of the 20th century, the sofa came loaded with symbolic baggage"

widened versions of armchair designs. This is the case for Austrian Josef Hoffmann's Kubus (*197: 5*), with a tufted leather design that applied the Vienna Secession founder's signature grid pattern to lounge furniture. In 1928, Le Corbusier, Pierre Jeanneret and Charlotte Perriand designed the first furniture collection in tubular steel, including the Fauteuil Grand Confort (*197: 9*) that was later produced as a sofa. The Tank sofa (*199: 21*) by Aino and Alvar Aalto is a stretched-out version of the Tank armchair with the same bentwood armrests. The Barcelona couch, a slim daybed in chromed steel and leather,

was adapted by Mies van der Rohe from his Barcelona chair. Ditto for the Womb sofa (*200: 28*), based on Eero Saarinen's cocoon-like armchair.

The disinterest in sofas is evident in the work of Florence Knoll, the first design director of US furniture firm Knoll. In the 1950s, the company worked with a stellar cast of designers including Saarinen and Van der Rohe. Florence Knoll self-deprecatingly called her own designs the "meat and potatoes" of the company and ended up drawing up most of the company's sofas because "no one else was designing [them]". Her upright, tufted designs, such as the Relaxed (*202: 37*) from 1954, remain the archetype of the mid-century sofa, equally as well-suited for the home as for a corporate lobby.

That is not to say that there were no early innovators. In the mid-1930s, émigré Austrian architect Friedrich Kiesler designed the Party Lounge (*200: 27*), a flat couch with ten black leather cushions, three of which could be lifted up to make a backrest. It could accommodate various lounging constellations and was easily converted into a two-person bed at the end of the night. In 1954, Charles and Ray Eames designed the Compact, a pared-back sofa that could easily be taken apart for a move. On both counts – the sofa bed and the modular couch – few designs have come close to the elegance of the originals.

A memorable if short-lived trend of the late 1950s was the conversation pit. It was popularised by Saarinen, who placed a sunken sofa in the middle of the living room of the now-iconic Miller House in Columbus, Indiana, in 1957. By 1963, *Time* magazine was declaring the fad to be over, citing the downsides of up-skirt views, hors d'oeuvres falling from above and the problem that "late-staying guests tended to fall in".

The golden age of 20th-century sofa design began around the late 1960s, in the sexual revolution. The straitlaced interiors of the modernists' International Style (think of Mies van der Rohe's austere glass pavilions) were declared passé and living rooms were again allowed to be comfortable, inviting and a little sultry. Sofas became deep-seated and low-slung. This era saw the birth of the quintessential Italian leather couch, so comfy it is near-impossible to get up

> "Sometime in the late 1960s, Piero Busnelli saw a foam bath duck and had the idea to apply the same material on the scale of a settee"

from once you have sunk into it, as well as many evergreen models including the Togo (*208: 70*) by Michel Ducaroy for Ligne Roset, the Camaleonda (*207: 63*) by Mario Bellini for B&B Italia, and the Soriana (*206: 59*) by Afra and Tobia Scarpa for Cassina.

For the 1972 exhibition *Italy: A New Domestic Landscape* at New York's Museum of Modern Art, Mario Bellini presented the Kar-a-Sutra, a jumbo car with interiors made up of rows of slouchy couches. The so-called "mobile human space" allowed passengers "to stretch out, sleep, smile, chat face-to-face, stand up, enjoy the sun, take photos, play cards, eat and drink, make love". This free-thinking spirit was adapted into a commercial product in the form of Le Bambole for B&B Italia, a modular series of plush couches that was launched alongside

an Oliviero Toscani advertising campaign in which Andy Warhol muse Donna Jordan was depicted splayed out on the couch in all possible orientations – and topless.

In the late 1960s, B&B Italia brought about a technological leap in the manufacture of sofas when it invented the use of cold-moulded polyurethane foam for furniture. Sometime in the mid 1960s, company founder Piero Busnelli saw a foam bath duck and had the idea of applying the same material to a settee. Soon it became possible to pour a synthetic foam into a mould of any shape, insert an iron frame, upholster it, and have a finished sofa – bypassing the costly and time-consuming traditional sofa construction methods using wood, springs and horsehair that had remained essentially unchanged since the Industrial Revolution. Not long after, B&B Italia was shipping vacuum-packed, inflatable foam loungers to customers – the Up collection by Gaetano Pesce – that were just the ticket at the height of the Space Age.

These manufacturing advancements, combined with the radical spirit of 1968, produced sofa experimentation not seen since 18th-century France. Italian collective Archizoom came up with the Superonda (*205: 52*), two foam cushions with wavy edges that could be slotted together into a rectangular mattress or arranged next to each other to form a curvy seat and backrest. Archizoom also created the faux fur-lined Safari (*206: 54*), which recreated the feeling of a conversation pit without the need for sunken floors. In South America, Chilean artist Roberto Matta designed the Malitte, a set of lounge furniture that could be slotted together, like a children's puzzle, into a big, soft square.

If the 1960s loosened the formal constraints around the sofa, they were fully untied by the arrival of postmodernism. This movement, which poked fun at the dictates of good taste, brought settees back to the frivolous and decorative function that they had played in European salons. In Gaetano Pesce's Tramonto a New York (or Sunset in New York, *210: 78*) from 1980, the cushions are shaped like skyscrapers while the backrest is a deep-orange sun. Hans Hollein's Marilyn (*210: 80*), also from the 1980s, directly references French 18th-century design in the form of a comically opulent fainting couch upholstered in baby-blue fabric.

Many artists also tried their hand at sofa design with surprisingly successful results. The Mae West Lips sofa, one of the most recognisable surrealist pieces, was born when Salvador Dalí had the idea to make a couch in the shape of the actress' mouth (it is still in production by BD Barcelona). In 1982, American minimalist artist Donald Judd drew inspiration from a high-backed Italian porter's sofa to design a bed with three high wooden sides, creating an intimate, confidential feeling for anyone lounging or sleeping in it. In 1991, Austrian artist Franz West created the Diwan, a couch as light as a daybed, which was built around the proportions of the body. Authorised reproductions of Judd's and West's designs are today sold by art galleries for five figures.

On a mass-consumption level throughout the 20th century, by far the largest influence on living rooms – and subsequently sofas – was television. The typical contemporary sofa, with its wide armrests and soft seats that invite you to curl up into them, only arrived around the same time that TVs started becoming widespread in homes and the living room was reoriented towards the screen. The all-American recliner armchairs and sofas – the memorable favourite of Joey in the sitcom *Friends* – are still some of the most popular sofas in the world. Just one recliner couch manufacturer, Hangzhou-based Kuka, produces 1.5 million of them per year, or about three every minute.

As the dominance of the TV has waned, the role of the sofa in the home has again become an open-ended question. It might be used for entertaining guests, watching Netflix alone, hosting people reading or on their phones, having friends crash overnight, or even as an occasional home office. This new need for flexibility is also reflected in the most recent crop of sofa designs. French-Canadian designer Willo Perron's Sausage is an 11-metre-long, floppy pillow that can snake around a room or be piled up in a cushion mountain. Another radically contemporary sofa is the Glade by Rick Owens: a huge sectional sofa with a high canopy that practically creates a room in itself. The musician Travis Scott has a custom Glade with a built-in recording studio, which he brings on tour, reassembling the lounge area backstage at each concert venue.

The design of the sofa – more than maybe any other kind of furniture – has always reflected society's shifting technological and cultural mores, from humanity's original decision to become domestic, through imperial decadence and industrialisation, all the way forward to the reign of digital screens. The surprisingly eclectic variations of the sofa include *canapés*, *caseuses* and *confidentiels*; divans, daybeds and fainting couches; sofa beds, sectionals and now sausages. Today, it is possible to choose a sofa the size of an entire room, one composed purely out of loose cushions or even a flat-pack Ikea number costing €129. And still, you can never go wrong with a Knole.

Stella Roos is Monocle's design correspondent. Originally from Helsinki, she has owned sofas in London and Berlin and is now looking to acquire one in New York.

A century (and a quarter) of sofa design
Virginia McLeod

In the following pages, we have selected 100 sofas representing the best from more than a century of sofa design – from the early 1900s to the 21st century. While any selection is subjective, this illustrated chronology nonetheless provides fascinating insights into the evolution of the sofa as a distinct item of furniture, as well as a who's who of furniture design. The majority were designed by architects who, as a profession, brought on the seismic changes that characterised 20th century design, developing furniture as a discrete discipline within key architectural movements. Contemporary architects continue to create some of the most intriguing sofas, alongside a new breed of talented furniture, interior and product designers, many of whom are profiled in these pages.

Sofa design has a history that tails back several centuries but it was at the turn of the 20th century that this particular piece of furniture underwent significant transformation. Prior to this point, furniture design was the domain of master craftsmen who specialised in the intricate arts of joinery, polishing, lacquering, inlaying, upholstery and other artisanal specialities. While styles and tastes came and went – usually at the behest of the monied, landed and titled classes – true innovation didn't arrive until the 1910s and 1920s when a handful of influential architects decided that everything that had gone before – from cities to furniture and everything in between – must be put out onto the curb and consigned to the landfill of design history.

As the decades progressed, industrialisation, two world wars, social upheavals and the breakneck speed of technological innovation drove these architects to use their skills to improve living conditions, especially in cities. In Europe housing had become a political and social scandal – crumbling residential stock, crowded living conditions and a lack of running water underpinned an endless cycle of ill health and poverty. Architects across the continent believed that they had the solution to all the mess, disease and ugliness and made it their business to sort it out.

This grand ambition meant that it was highly unlikely that those pursuing this cause would stop at the architecture. Or even the interiors. Rather, this new generation of designers took over every facet of design in the domestic realm. The old, heavy, dusty and overstuffed furniture that had crowded living spaces in the preceding decades was deemed entirely unsuitable for the light, bright, health-promoting houses and apartments that were being envisioned. Everything was examined and found wanting – lighting, textiles, cutlery, crockery (indeed entire kitchens). Furniture, naturally, was reinvented from scratch.

The Vienna Secessionists got a head start on this revolution by resigning from the Association of Austrian Artists in 1897 in protest against traditional styles. Architects Josef Hoffmann (*page 196: sofa 1 & page 197: sofa 5*) and Otto Wagner (*196: 2*) produced astounding works of both architecture and furniture, many of which are still in production today. Hoffmann went on to found the Wiener Werkstätte ("Vienna Workshop") in 1903, and while the architects and artists of the Werkstätte primarily focused on textiles, jewellery, leather goods and ceramics, it was at this time that Hoffmann and Wagner produced sofas and other furniture as part of their private architectural commissions.

Germany's Bauhaus, much influenced by the Wiener Werkstätte, was next in line. Founded by Berlin-born architect Walter Gropius in 1919, this group and school, which combined arts and manufacturing, produced a stunning array of furniture that aligned with its mission to strip away unnecessary decoration and embrace mass-production materials and processes. The furniture that was produced during the Bauhaus school's short existence (it lasted just 14 years before being shut down by the Nazi regime in 1933) remains enormously influential nearly 100 years later. Sofas and other furniture by Bauhaus architects, including Walter Gropius (*197: 6*), Mies van der Rohe (*205: 51*) and Marcel Breuer (*198: 14* and *200: 23*), have stood the test of time and are still highly collectible design icons.

Elsewhere in Europe, Swiss-born, Paris-based renegade Charles Édouard Jeanneret-Gris – or Le Corbusier – sought to address societal problems through his design work, using the opportunity presented by his private residential commissions. For these projects he would create all manner of tables, chairs and sofas that reflected his belief that furniture must serve human needs in its utility, proportion and harmony. One sofa that resulted, the Fauteuil Grand Confort (*197: 09*) is another 20th-century icon. Le Corbusier's close collaborators Charlotte Perriand and Pierre Jeanneret – who were credited with the authorship of the Grand Confort alongside him – produced other now-iconic furniture designs of their own, such as the Capitol Complex sofa by

"This new generation of designers took over every facet of design in the domestic realm. The old, heavy, dusty furniture was deemed entirely unsuitable"

Jeanneret (*202: 35*) and the 514 Refolo sofa by Perriand (*202: 34*).

Meanwhile, further north in Europe, the 1940s and 1950s saw Copenhagen-based architects take centre stage as they too reinvented architecture and design in a bid to create better, more affordable and more beautiful living environments. The ensuing, prolific mid-century Danish design movement saw furniture overtake architecture as the primary vehicle for invention. Architects including Finn Juhl (*200: 28* and *201: 32*), Arne Jacobsen (*203: 41*), Bruno Mathsson (*200: 27*) and Verner Panton (*207: 62*) designed sofas that reflected their commitment to sustaining the country's craft traditions (woodworking in particular). This cohort created unique designs that were functional, elegant and catered to the

human form. And while much of the furniture that characterises the resulting Danish modern period was designed by architects, they did so alongside a number of dedicated furniture and product designers – including, notably, Hans Wegner (*202: 36*) who, while not a trained architect, built an extraordinary catalogue of furniture and without whom even the briefest account of Danish design would not be complete. This period in Denmark remains enormously influential and is unsurpassed in its originality and influence on the architects and designers who followed them.

Much of the furniture and homeware designed by the Danes in the mid-century period – and indeed more than a few of the architects and designers themselves – made their way to the US in the postwar period, where their sofas, chairs, tables, sideboards, lamps, cutlery and chinaware gained enormous popularity. These in turn influenced another groundbreaking architecture movement now known as mid-century modern. American architects – and a number of newly arrived Europeans who had emigrated before or after the Second World War – found fertile creative ground on both coasts of America. California was particularly fruitful, with creatives producing simple, elegant and radical furniture that perfectly accompanied the glass-and-steel houses that were springing up across Los Angeles, Palm Springs and elsewhere along the west coast. Architects including Charles and Ray Eames (*211: 84*), Warren Platner (*205: 50*) and Adrian Pearsall (*203: 43*) as well as legendary designer and entrepreneur Florence Knoll (*202: 37*) created popular furniture, much of which is still in demand more than 75 years later.

Back in Europe, the Italians were, as ever, going their own inimitable way. From the late 1960s the Radical Design movement, which developed in Florence, Milan and Turin, saw architects wholeheartedly reject the rationalism and insistence on function that modernism had promoted. Instead, it embraced unconventional materials and forms to create visually striking sofas and other furniture. Groups of architect collaborators, including Archizoom Associati (*205: 52* and *206: 54*) and the Memphis Group, which was founded by Ettore Sottsass (*204: 44*) in 1980 and also included Michele De Lucchi (*210: 82*), left an indelible mark on the sofa landscape. Other legendary Italian architects of the 1970s and 1980s – now recognised as among the greatest furniture designers in the world, including Alessandro Mendini (*209: 77*), Marco Zanuso (*201: 33*), Mario Bellini (*207: 63*) and Gaetano Pesce (*210: 78*) – produced playful, experimental and sometimes politically charged furniture.

The influence of these Italian architects was global and fuelled an international postmodern style that similarly rejected modernism and its constraints. In the US and in the UK, architects and designers produced works that referenced the classical architecture of the ancient Greeks and Romans. This late flowering (some would argue deterioration) of postmodernism ushered in the demise of officially recognised styles and movements in architecture (and consequentially furniture design), aside from the last formally recognised movement: deconstructivism. Architects associated with the deconstructivist movement, which proliferated in the 1980s and 1990s, while not necessarily accepting the label themselves, include Frank Gehry (*213: 93*) and Zaha Hadid (*212: 88*). In the same period, pioneering French architect and industrial designer Philippe Starck (*213: 95*) took a different tack. Known for the sense of humour he brings to his work, his sofas are as good examples as any of the appliance of whimsy and humour in furniture design.

And so to the 21st century and the sofa design work taking place today. The Austrians, Germans, Danes, Italians and Americans cited above still exert a profound influence on the architects and designers who are creating furniture in the 2020s and beyond. For proof of this reach, one only has to look at the many sofas, chairs and tables – created in what can now be seen as a profoundly creative century – which are still in production and also remain in great demand on the vintage market.

The architects designing furniture today are no longer clustered into defined geographical or cultural enclaves. Still, countries like Italy and Denmark have an appreciation for furniture design so embedded in their contemporary national identities that a new generation of young designers has picked up the baton. Elsewhere, architects with global practices are designing sofas for an international market and exploring new materials and technologies, while placing sustainability at the top of the agenda. These include Norman Foster (*214: 97*), Antonio Citterio (*213: 91*), David Chipperfield (*213: 90*), Patricia Urquiola (*215: 99*), Thomas Heatherwick (*215: 100*) and designer Marcel Wanders (*214: 96*), all of whom bring international sensibilities and sophisticated technologies to their sofa offerings. But back to the beginning we must now travel – with a chronological illustrated survey of 100 sofas from the past 100 (and 25) years.

Virginia McLeod brings her training as an architect and passion for modern and contemporary design to her role as head of book publishing at Monocle.

100 sofas:
An illustrated chronology

Fledermaus sofa
1905

Designer: *Josef Hoffmann*
Manufacturer: *J & J Kohn (initial production), Thonet*

Bentwood sofa
1905

Designer: *Otto Wagner*
Manufacturer: *Thonet*

Batlló bench
1906

Designer: *Antoni Gaudí*
Manufacturer: *Casas i Bardés (original), BD Barcelona*

Thonet (founded 1819)

One of the most influential furniture companies in the world, Thonet is famous for revolutionising the production of bentwood furniture. The company traces its origins to 1819, when cabinetmaker Michael Thonet opened a workshop in Boppard, Germany. He experimented with bending solid wood using steam – a technique that would change the face of furniture design. In the 20th century Thonet collaborated with designers of the Vienna Secession including Otto Wagner (his bentwood sofa is pictured above) and later with architects from the Bauhaus to produce tubular steel furniture.

Robie 3 sofa
1908

Designer: *Frank Lloyd Wright*
Manufacturer: *Heinz & Co (initial production), Cassina*

Kubus sofa
1910

Designer: *Josef Hoffmann*
Manufacturer: *Wittmann*

F51-3 sofa
1920s

Designer: *Walter Gropius*
Manufacturer: *Tecta*

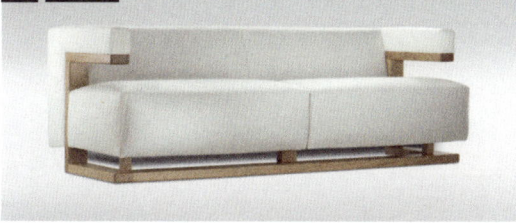

Samsas sofa
1923

Designer: *Carl Malmsten*
Manufacturer: *O H Sjögren
(redesign in 1960)*

Lota sofa
1924

Designer: *Eileen Gray*
Manufacturer: *ClassiCon*

**Fauteuil
Grand Confort**
1928

Designers: *Le Corbusier, Pierre
Jeanneret, Charlotte Perriand*
Manufacturer: *Cassina*

Cassina (founded 1927)

With a back catalogue that includes collaborations with
some of the world's best architects, Cassina rose to global
prominence in the 1950s working with leading Italian
designers such as Vico Magistretti, Mario Bellini and
Gio Ponti. In the 1960s, Cassina started reissuing classic
furniture by the early modernists including Le Corbusier,
Pierre Jeanneret and Charlotte Perriand (their Grand
Confort sofa is pictured above). It's an industry-shaping
legacy that continues into the 21st century under the
artistic direction of Patricia Urquiola.

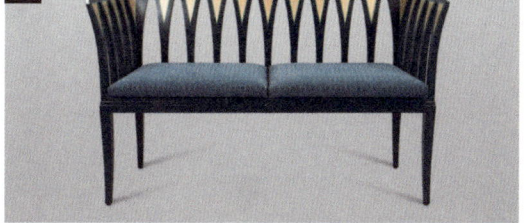

Blue sofa
1929

Designer: *Eliel Saarinen*
Manufacturer: *Adelta Oy (reissue)*

Alpha sofa
1929

Designer: *Richard Neutra*
Manufacturer: *VS*

197

Art deco sofa
1930

Designer: *H Pander & Zonen*
Manufacturer: *H Pander & Zonen*

Bauhaus sofa
1930

Designer: *Hynek Gottwald*
Manufacturer: *Hynek Gottwald*

Couch
1931

Designer: *Marcel Breuer*
Manufacturer: *Tecta*

T33 sofa
1933

Designer: *Franco Albini*
Manufacturer: *Officina della Scala*

Utrecht sofa
1935

Designer: *Gerrit Rietveld*
Manufacturer: *Cassina*

TMBO sofa
1935

Designer: *Magnus Læssøe Stephensen*
Manufacturer: *Mazo*

5011 sofa
1935

Designer: *Kaare Klint*
Manufacturer: *Rud Rasmussen*

Pretzel sofa
1935

Designer: *Paul T Frankl*
Manufacturer: *Private commission*

Vilhelm sofa
1935

Designer: *Flemming Lassen*
Manufacturer: *Audo Copenhagen
(current reissue)*

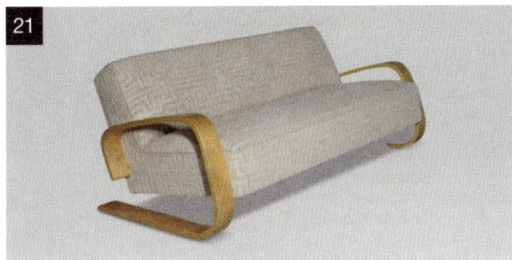

Tank sofa
1936

Designer: *Alvar Aalto*
Manufacturer: *Artek*

Party Lounge sofa
1936

Designer: *Friedrich Kiesler*
Manufacturer: *Wittmann*

Devalle sofa
1939

Designer: *Carlo Mollino*
Manufacturer: *Private commission, Galleria Colombari (reissue)*

Breuer 2 Seater sofa
1936

Designer: *Marcel Breuer*
Manufacturer: *Isokon Plus*

 **1940s**

Fiorenza sofa
1940

Designer: *Franco Albini*
Manufacturer: *Prototype*

Little Petra VB2 sofa
1938

Designer: *Viggo Boesen*
Manufacturer: *&Tradition (update based on original drawings)*

Eva sofa
1941

Designer: *Bruno Mathsson*
Manufacturer: *Firma Karl Mathsson*

&Tradition (founded 2010)

Copenhagen-based &Tradition bridges the divide between tradition and innovation. Since 2010, the company has been reissuing classic Danish furniture and lighting by the likes of Arne Jacobsen, Verner Panton, Jørn Utzon and Viggo Boesen (his sofa is pictured above), while simultaneously acting as a champion and collaboration partner for 21st-century talent. International designers including Jaime Hayon, Industrial Facility and Luca Nichetto work with &Tradition on everything from accessories and lighting to furniture.

Womb sofa
1948

Designer: *Eero Saarinen*
Manufacturer: *Knoll*

Chieftain sofa
1949

Designer: *Finn Juhl*
Manufacturer: *Niels Vodder*
(original), *House of Finn Juhl*

Belladonna sofa
1951

Designer: *Franco Albini*
and Franca Helg
Manufacturer: *Sika Design*

1950s

Capri sofa
1950

Designer: *Johannes Andersen*
Manufacturer: *Trensums*

Baker sofa
1951

Designer: *Finn Juhl*
Manufacturer: *Baker Furniture*
(original), *House of Finn Juhl*

Lady sofa
1951

Designer: *Marco Zanuso*
Manufacturer: *Arflex*

514 Refolo sofa
1953

Designer: *Charlotte Perriand*
Manufacturer: *Cassina*

**Capitol
Complex sofa**
1953

Designer: *Pierre Jeanneret*
Manufacturer: *Produced in India
(original), Cassina*

GE-290/3 sofa
1953

Designer: *Hans Wegner*
Manufacturer: *Getama*

Relaxed sofa
1954

Designer: *Florence Knoll*
Manufacturer: *Knoll*

Knoll (founded 1938)

A legend in the world of furniture design, founder Hans
Knoll, later joined in 1941 by architect Florence Knoll,
introduced the aesthetics of modernist European design,
in particular the Bauhaus principles, to a US audience.
Florence Knoll (her Relaxed sofa is pictured above)
established the design direction, and her collaborations
with émigrés including Mies van der Rohe, Eero Saarinen
and Harry Bertoia resulted in some of the postwar
period's most iconic furniture. Today Knoll works with
the likes of Ini Archibong, Jay Osgerby and Marc Newson
who continue the brand's illustrious design legacy.

Bench No 356
1956

Designer: *Jean Prouvé*
Manufacturer: *Atelier Jean Prouvé*

Due Foglie sofa
1957

Designer: *Gio Ponti*
Manufacturer: *Molteni&C*

Molteni&C (founded 1934)

A family-run business for three generations, Molteni&C began life as an artisan furniture workshop before embracing postwar industrial production. Its approach to craftsmanship has struck the balance between tradition and quality. Since 2016, under the creative direction of Vincent Van Duysen, the company has reissued furniture by the legendary Gio Ponti (his sofa is pictured above), as well as collaborating with architects including Jean Nouvel, Foster + Partners and Herzog & de Meuron to bring understated luxury with an architectural sensibility to the company's collections.

Widdicomb sofa
1958

Designer: *George Nakashima*
Manufacturer: *Widdicomb-Mueller*

Swan sofa
1958

Designer: *Arne Jacobsen*
Manufacturer: *Fritz Hansen*

Fritz Hansen (founded 1872)

Danish brand Fritz Hansen is best known for its partnership with architect Arne Jacobsen, with whom it produced furniture that is as popular today as when it launched in the 1950s – including the Swan Chair (in its sofa edition pictured above). Established in the late 1800s by cabinetmaker Fritz Hansen, the early reputation of the company was built on steam-bent wood furniture, but its record from the postwar period was secured with long-running collaborations with Jacobsen, as well as Verner Panton and Poul Kjaerholm, and more lately with a roster of international designers.

Tuxedo Loveseat sofa
1960

Designer: *Gordon Bunshaft and Davis Allen*
Manufacturer: *Thonet Industries USA*

Platform 2006-S sofa
1960s

Designer: *Adrian Pearsall*
Manufacturer: *Craft Associates*

Califfo sofa
1962

Designer: *Ettore Sottsass*
Manufacturer: *Poltronova*

Djinn sofa
1963

Designer: *Olivier Mourgue*
Manufacturer: *Air Borne*

620 sofa
1962

Designer: *Dieter Rams*
Manufacturer: *Vitsoe*

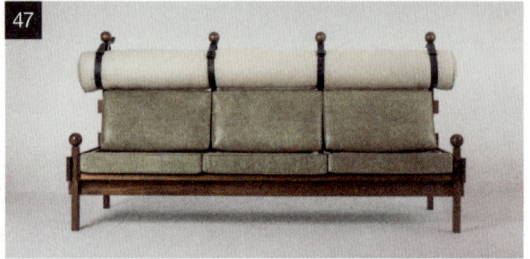

Tonico sofa
1963

Designer: *Sergio Rodrigues*
Manufacturer: *OCA Meia-Pataca*

Saratoga sofa
1964

Designer: *Lella and Massimo Vignelli*
Manufacturer: *Poltronova*

Rodeio sofa
1965

Designer: *Jean Gillon*
Manufacturer: *Italma Woodart*

**Model
No. 263 sofa**
1967

Designer: *Mies van der Rohe*
Manufacturer: *Knoll*

Platner sofa
1966

Designer: *Warren Platner*
Manufacturer: *Knoll*

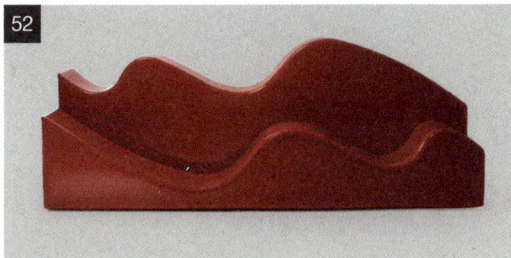

Superonda sofa
1967

Designer: *Archizoom Associati*
Manufacturer: *Poltronova*

Basket sofa
1967

Designer: *Joe Colombo*
Manufacturer: *Bonacina (original)*, *Gubi*

54

Safari sofa
1968

Designer: *Archizoom Associati*
Manufacturer: *Poltronova*

58

ABCD
3-Seater sofa
1968

Designer: *Pierre Paulin*
Manufacturer: *Artifort*

55

Sofa/daybed
1968

Designer: *Egon Eiermann*
Manufacturer: *Honeta*

59

Soriana sofa
1969

Designer: *Afra and Tobia Scarpa*
Manufacturer: *Cassina*

56

Sacco sofa
1968

Designer: *Piero Gatti, Cesare Paolini, Franco Teodoro*
Manufacturer: *Zanotta*

60

Serpente sofa
1969

Designer: *Marzio Cecchi*
Manufacturer: *Studio Most*

57

Silver Series sofa
1968

Designer: *Eero Aarnio*
Manufacturer: *Mobel Italia*

61

Vario Pillo sofa
1969

Designer: *Burkhard Vogtherr*
Manufacturer: *Rosenthal*

Cloverleaf sofa
1969

Designer: *Verner Panton*
Manufacturer: *Verpan*

Tucroma sofa
1971

Designer: *Guido Faleschini*
Manufacturer: *i4 Mariani*

Camaleonda Modular sofa
1970

Designer: *Mario Bellini*
Manufacturer: *B&B Italia*

Coupé sofa model 2292
1971

Designer: *Børge Mogensen*
Manufacturer: *Fredericia Furniture*

B&B Italia (founded 1966)

From the beginning B&B Italia embraced modern production techniques including pioneering the use of cold-moulded polyurethane used in upholstered furniture, enabling designers to be more adventurous. Mario Bellini (his Camaleonda sofa is pictured above) took full advantage of this technique, as did Gaetano Pesce, both designers challenging conventions in furniture design. The company now partners with leading international designers including Michael Anastassiades and Naoto Fukasawa. B&B Italia remains at the top of its game and an enduring symbol of Italian design.

Fredericia Furniture (founded 1911)

The company takes its name from the town of Fredericia on the Jutland peninsula in Denmark. Originally a small, traditional manufacturer of high-quality furniture, the company was transformed when it partnered with leading mid-century Danish designer Børge Mogensen (his Coupé sofa is pictured above). Fredericia has been a cornerstone of postwar Danish design, a position it still occupies today, reinforced by new collaborations with the likes of Jasper Morrison and Cecilie Manz, each collection reflecting the brand's values of craftsmanship and human-centred design.

Cube sofa
1970

Designer: *Jorge Zalszupin*
Manufacturer: *L'Atelier Móveis*

Zeppelin sofa
1972

Designer: *Walter Leeman*
Manufacturer: *Velda*

Confidential sofa
1972

Designer: *Alberto Rosselli*
Manufacturer: *Saporiti*

DS-1025 Terrazza sofa
1973

Designer: *Ubald Klug*
Manufacturer: *De Sede*

Togo sofa
1973

Designer: *Michel Ducaroy*
Manufacturer: *Ligne Roset*

Maralunga sofa
1973

Designer: *Vico Magistretti*
Manufacturer: *Cassina*

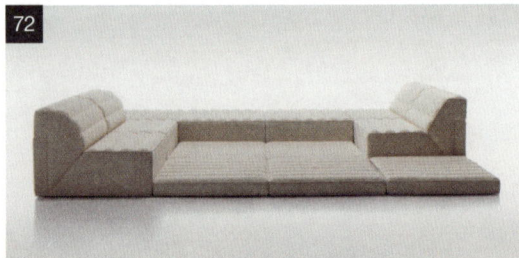

Free System sofa
1973

Designer: *Claudio Salocchi*
Manufacturer: *Acerbis*

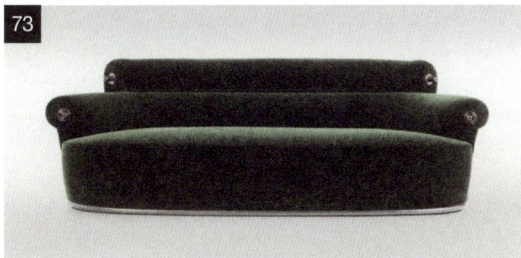

73

Toro sofa
1973

Designer: *Luigi Caccia Dominioni*
Manufacturer: *Azucena*

75

Bogo sofa
1976

Designer: *Carlo Bartoli*
Manufacturer: *Rossi di Albizzate*

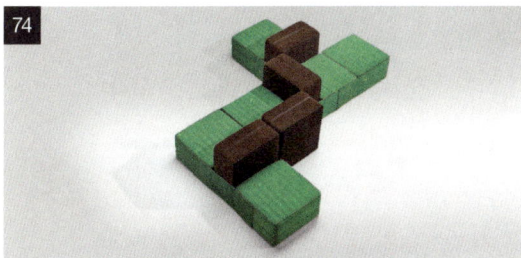

74

Settebello
1974

Designer: *De Pas, D'Urbino
& Lomazzi*
Manufacturer: *Zanotta*

76

Brigadier sofa
1978

Designer: *Cini Boeri*
Manufacturer: *Knoll*

77

Kandissi sofa
1978

Designer: *Alessandro Mendini*
Manufacturer: *Studio Alchimia*

Tramonto a New York
1980

Designer: *Gaetano Pesce*
Manufacturer: *Cassina*

79

ON sofa
1980

Designer: *Oscar Niemeyer*
Manufacturer: *Etel (reissue)*

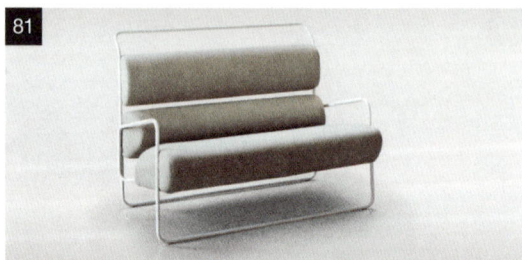

81

Sancarlo sofa
1982

Designer: *Achille Castiglioni*
Manufacturer: *Driade (original)*,
Tacchini

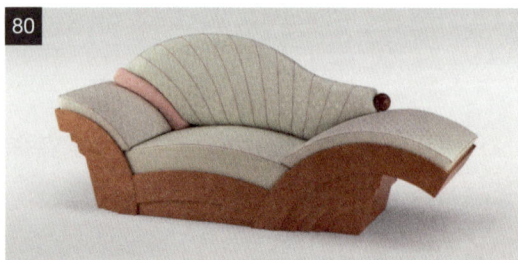

80

Marilyn sofa
1980

Designer: *Hans Hollein*
Manufacturer: *Poltronova*

82

Lido sofa
1982

Designer: *Michele De Lucchi*
Manufacturer: *Memphis Milano*

Obliqua sofa
1983

Designer: *Mario Botta*
Manufacturer: *Alias*

ES 108 Three-Seat sofa
1984

Designer: *Charles & Ray Eames*
Manufacturer: *Herman Miller*

Herman Miller (founded 1905)

Herman Miller started life as the Star Furniture Company in Michigan. Herman Miller, an early investor, renamed the company in 1923 and appointed his son-in-law DJ De Pree as managing director. De Pree moved the company's production from traditional to modern design and this transformation accelerated in the 1940s through collaborations with architects and designers such as George Nelson, Charles and Ray Eames (their sofa pictured above) and Isamu Noguchi. Today, its roster of celebrated international designers includes the likes of Ilse Crawford and Keiji Takeuchi.

How High the Moon sofa
1986

Designer: *Shiro Kuramata*
Manufacturer: *Terada Tekkojo for Idée*

Walse sofa
1986

Designer: *Tito Agnoli*
Manufacturer: *Poltrona Frau*

Poltrona Frau (founded 1912)

Poltrona ("armchair" in Italian) Frau was founded by Renzo Frau in Turin, where, in the early 20th century, the company furnished luxury liners, hotels and royal residences in classic Italian styles. Known for its mastery in saddle leather and hand-finished upholstery, the company evolved by embracing innovation while preserving traditional craftsmanship. Collaborations with designers including Gio Ponti, Michele De Lucchi and Tito Agnoli (his sofa is pictured above) helped define the modern Italian style, a tradition continued today by designers including Kensaku Oshiro and Draga & Aurel.

Raffles sofa
1988

Designer: *Vico Magistretti*
Manufacturer: *De Padova*

De Padova (founded 1956)

The company started up as an importer of Scandinavian furniture in the mid-1950s, a bold move at a time when traditional Italian styles dominated the market. But the intrepid decision-making continued and saw De Padova launching its own collections in the 1960s that blended its Nordic simplicity with Italian craftsmanship. Their Milan showroom on Corso Venezia became a creative hub for the design crowd in the 1960s, and in the decades since, the company has collaborated with an impressive line-up of designers including Vico Magistretti (his sofa is pictured above), Dieter Rams and Achille Castiglioni.

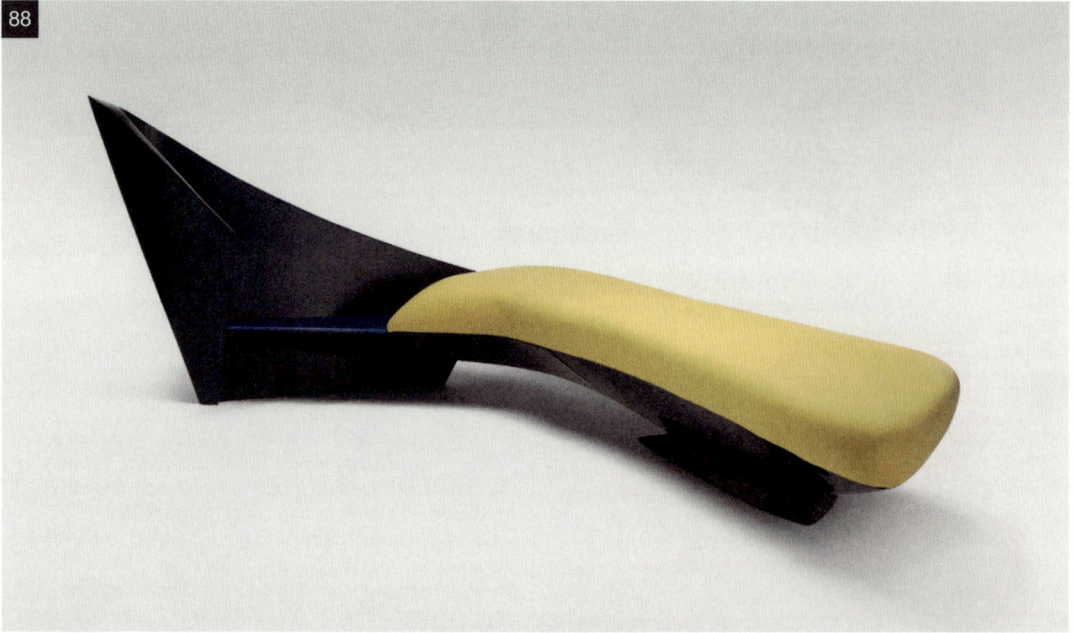

Wave sofa
1988

Designer: *Zaha Hadid*
Manufacturer: *Edra*

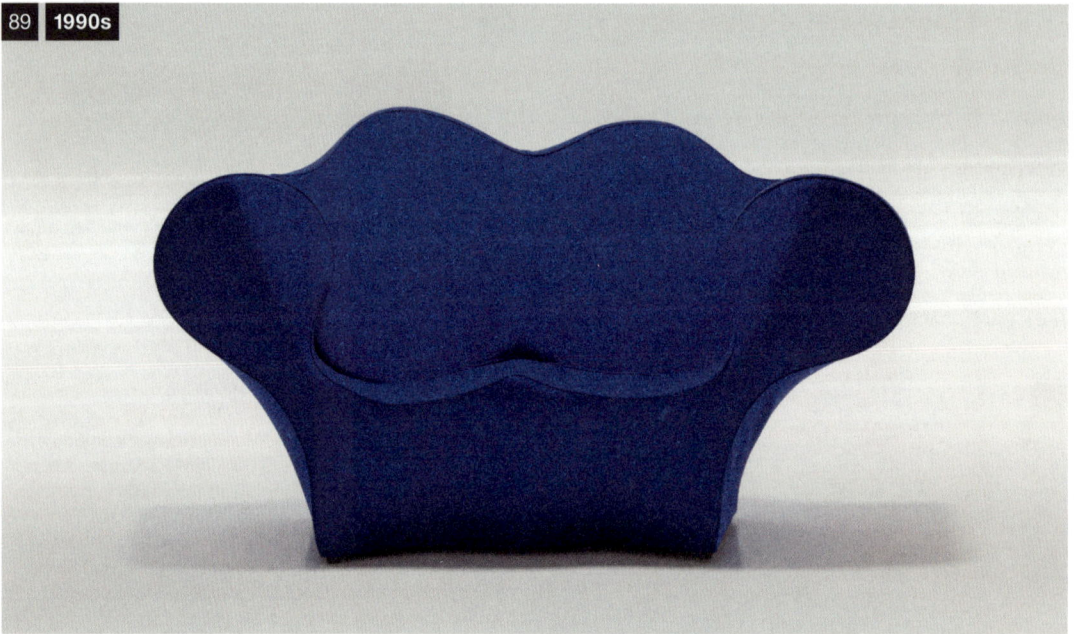

89 | 1990s

Double Soft Big Easy
1991

Designer: *Ron Arad*
Manufacturer: *Moroso*

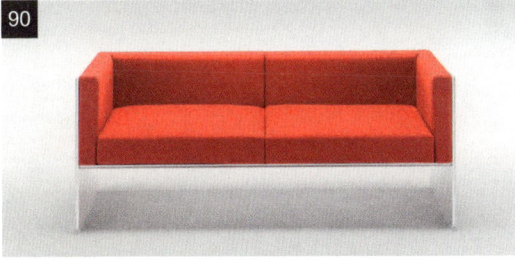

Air Frame sofa
1992

Designer: *David Chipperfield*
Manufacturer: *Cassina*

91 | 2000s

Groundpiece sofa
2001

Designer: *Antonio Citterio*
Manufacturer: *Flexform*

Flexform (founded 1959)

Located in the heart of Italy's furniture-making region of Brianza, Flexform was originally set up in the late 1950s as a small artisan workshop that gained a reputation for refined upholstery before embarking on a series of successful collaborations with the likes of Joe Colombo and Asnago Vender. The 1970s marked a turning point when architect Antonio Citterio began a long-term partnership with the firm (one of his many designs for the company is pictured above), defining Flexform's distinctive style and developing luxurious sofas and modular seating systems that remain at the heart of the company's brand.

Tokyo-Pop sofa
2002

Designer: *Tokujin Yoshioka*
Manufacturer: *Driade*

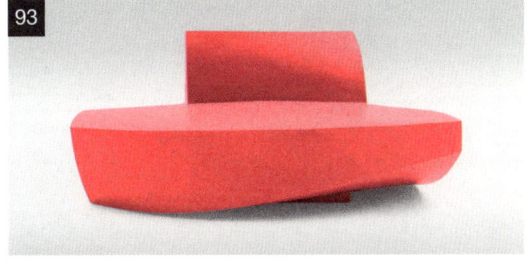

Gehry sofa
2004

Designer: *Frank Gehry*
Manufacturer: *Heller*

Filo sofa
2009

Designer: *Barber Osgerby*
Manufacturer: *Cappellini (private commission)*

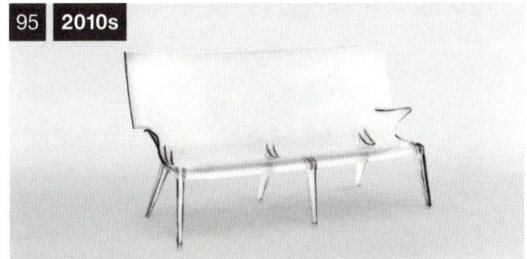

95 | 2010s

Uncle Jack sofa
2014

Designer: *Philippe Starck*
Manufacturer: *Kartell*

Kartell (founded 1949)

Engineer Giulio Castelli founded Kartell with a vision of applying cutting-edge industrial plastics to everyday products. Originally focused on the automotive industry, the company shifted to furniture in the 1960s and earned a global reputation for its bold experimental designs. Under the creative direction of Anna Castelli Ferrieri, Kartell became synonymous with contemporary Italian design, merging technology with style. Pieces such as the Ghost chair by Philippe Starck (another of his transparent pieces is pictured above) have become modern classics and reflect the company's innovative spirit.

Mad Chaise Longue 2016 — Designer: *Marcel Wanders* / Manufacturer: *Poliform*

Foster 620 bench 2018 — Designer: *Norman Foster* / Manufacturer: *Walter Knoll*

Poliform (founded 1970)

Evolving from a family-run workshop in Brianza, a region known for its furniture-making heritage, Poliform gained a reputation for quality storage systems and wardrobes, expanding into complete home solutions including kitchens, beds and complementary furniture with a strong architectural sensibility. In the 1990s the takeover of a dedicated kitchen brand saw the consolidation of its reputation for home systems. Over the decades the company has forged collaborations with acclaimed designers such as Carlo Colombo, Paolo Piva and Dutch designer Marcel Wanders – his chaise sofa is pictured above.

Walter Knoll (founded 1865)

In 1865 Wilhelm Knoll opened a leather shop in Stuttgart, establishing what would become a world-leading family-run furniture dynasty. It rose to prominence in the early 20th century with groundbreaking designs, such as the lightweight Prodomo armchair, created under the watch of second-generation Walter Knoll (his son, Hans, would establish Knoll in the US). Highlights include furnishing apartments designed by Ludwig Mies van der Rohe and kitting out Berlin's famed Tegel Airport. Today, it continues to work with the world's best designers and architects, including Norman Foster and Kengo Kuma.

98 | 2020s

Wireframe sofa 2020 — Designer: *Industrial Facility* / Manufacturer: *Herman Miller*

Dudet sofa
2024

Designer: *Patricia Urquiola*
Manufacturer: *Cassina*

In-side sofa
2024

Designer: *Thomas Heatherwick*
Manufacturer: *Magis*

Directory of designers

Australia

**David Caon
& Jeramie Hotz**
Caon Design Office,
Sydney
caondesignoffice.com
— Page 010

Tamsin Johnson
Tamsin Johnson, Sydney
tamsinjohnson.com
— Page 156

John Wardle
Wardle, Melbourne
wardle.studio
— Page 038

**David Welsh &
Chris Major**
Welsh + Major, Sydney
welshmajor.com
— Page 140

Belgium

**Fien Muller &
Hannes Van Severen**
Muller Van Severen, Ghent
mullervanseveren.be
— Page 144

Brazil

Marcio Kogan
Studio MK27, São Paulo
mk27.com
— Page 022

Canada

Brigitte Shim
Shim-Sutcliffe Architects,
Toronto
shim-sutcliffe.com
— Page 032

Chile

Rodrigo Bravo
Bravo Estudio, Santiago
bravo.io
— Page 094

China

Betty Ng
Collective, Hong Kong
collective-studio.co
— Page 048

Joyce Wang
Joyce Wang, Hong Kong
joycewangstudio.com
— Page 164

Denmark

Bjarke Ingels
BIG, Copenhagen
big.dk
— Page 014

Dorte Mandrup
Dorte Mandrup,
Copenhagen
dortemandrup.dk
— Page 160

David Thulstrup
David Thulstrup,
Copenhagen
davidthulstrup.com
— Page 134

France

Ronan Bouroullec
Ronan & Erwan
Bouroullec, Paris
bouroullec.com
— Page 170

Joris Poggioli
Joris Poggioli, Paris
jorispoggioli.com
— Page 046

Germany

Sigurd Larsen
Sigurd Larsen Design,
Berlin
sigurdlarsen.com
— Page 154

India

Rahul Mehrotra
RMA Architects, Mumbai
rmaarchitects.com
— Page 124

Italy

Federica Biasi
Federica Biasi, Milan
federicabiasi.com
— Page 166

Patricia Urquiola
Studio Urquiola, Milan
patriciaurquiola.com
— Page 036

Japan

Keiji Ashizawa
KAD, Tokyo
keijidesign.com
— Page 112

Naoto Fukasawa
Naoto Fukasawa Design,
Tokyo
naotofukasawa.com
— Page 074

Yuko Nagayama
Yuko Nagayama and
Associates, Tokyo
yukonagayama.co.jp
— Page 106

Mexico

Tatiana Bilbao
Tatiana Bilbao Estudio,
Mexico City
tatianabilbao.com
— Page 108

Fernanda Canales
Fernanda Canales
Architecture, Mexico City
fernandacanales.com
— Page 150

Netherlands

Sabine Marcelis
Studio Sabine Marcelis,
Rotterdam
sabinemarcelis.com
— Page 042

Nigeria

Nifemi Marcus-Bello
Nmbello Studio, Lagos
nmbello.com
— Page 120

Tosin Oshinowo
Oshinowo Studio, Lagos
oshinowostudio.com
— Page 088

Portugal

Gabriel Tan
Origin Made, Porto
origin-made.com
— Page 018

Singapore

**Hunn Wai &
Olivia Lee**
Lanzavecchia + Wai,
Olivia Lee Studio,
Singapore
lanzavecchia-wai.com
olivia-lee.com
— Page 138

Switzerland

Ini Archibong
Design by Ini, Neuchâtel
designbyini.com
— Page 024

Thomas Hildebrand
Hildebrand, Zürich
hildebrand.ch
— Page 116

**Yuichi Kodai &
Claudia Maggi**
Kodai and Associates,
Zürich
kodaiandassociates.com
— Page 076

Thailand

**Chatpong
Chuenrudeemol**
Chat Architects, Bangkok
— Page 130

United Arab Emirates

Nada Debs
Studio Nada Debs, Dubai
nadadebs.com
— Page 066

United Kingdom

Ilse Crawford
Studioilse, London
studioilse.com
— Page 080

Yinka Ilori
Yinka Ilori, London
yinkailori.com
— Page 060

Niall Maxwell
Rural Office, Wales
rural-office.co.uk
— Page 146

Jasper Morrison
Jasper Morrison, London
jaspermorrison.com
— Page 090

Farshid Moussavi
Farshid Moussavi
Architecture, London
farshidmoussavi.com
— Page 052

Jay Osgerby
Barber Osgerby, London
barberosgerby.com
— Page 070

**Grant Wilkinson
& Teresa Rivera**
Wilkinson & Rivera,
London
wilkinson-rivera.com
— Page 178

USA

**Amale Andraos
& Dan Wood**
WorkAC, New York
work.ac
— Page 028

**Angie Brooks
& Lawrence Scarpa**
Brooks + Scarpa,
Los Angeles
brooksscarpa.com
— Page 084

Eran Chen
ODA, New York
oda-architecture.com
— Page 056

**Steven Holl &
Dimitra Tsachrelia**
Steven Holl Architects,
New York
stevenholl.com
— Page 062

Mariam Issoufou
Mariam Issoufou,
New York
mariamissoufou.com
— Page 126

Daniel Libeskind
Studio Libeskind,
New York
libeskind.com
— Page 102

Eric Owen Moss
Eric Owen Moss
Architects, Los Angeles
ericowenmoss.com
— Page 098

Alex Mustonen
Snarkitecture, New York
snarkitecture.com
— Page 180

Alfredo Paredes
Alfredo Paredes Studio,
New York
alfredoparedesstudio.com
— Page 174

Directory of sofas

Alfredo Paredes Studio
alfredoparedesstudio.com

Santana sofa, 2021
Designed by Alfredo Paredes
— Page 174

Arflex
arflex.it

Marenco sofa, 1970
Designed by Mario Marenco
— Page 048

BD Barcelona
bdbarcelona.com

Pillow sofa, 2020
Designed by
Muller Van Severen
— Page 144

Blu Dot
bludot.com

Sunday sofa, 2018
Designed by Blu Dot
— Page 180

Brdr Krüger
brdr-kruger.com

Karm sofa, 2018
Designed by
David Thulstrup
— Page 134

Cappellini
cappellini.com

Elan sofa, 1999
Designed by Jasper Morrison
— Page 070

Cassina
cassina.com

Maralunga sofa, 1973
Designed by Vico Magistretti
— Page 010

Dudet Bold sofa, 2025
Designed by
Patricia Urquiola
— Page 036

CB2
cb2.com

Strato sofa, 2020
Designed by Mermelada
Estudio
— Page 126

Crate & Barrel
crateandbarrel.com

Aidan sofa, 2014
Designed by Crate & Barrel
— Page 088

De Sede
desede.ch

DS-80 daybed, 1969
Designed by De Sede
— Page 116

Ecart International
ecart.paris

Club sofa, 1930
Designed by
Jean-Michel Frank
— Page 062

Flexform
flexform.it

Soft Dream sofa, 2010
Designed by Antonio Citterio
— Page 108

Formel A
formela.dk

A Sofa, 2017
Designed by Sigurd Larsen
— Page 154

France & Daverkosen

FD147L sofa, 1951
Designed by Hvidt
& Mølgaard
— Page 146

Fredericia
fredericia.com

Jota sofa, 2024
Designed by Jasper Morrison
— Page 090

George Smith
georgesmith.com

Ilse sofa, 2005
Designed by Ilse Crawford
— Page 080

Hay
hay.com

Can sofa, 2016
Designed by Ronan
& Erwan Bouroullec
— Page 094

Herman Miller
hermanmiller.com

Luva sofa, 2020
Designed by Gabriel Tan
— Page 018

House of Finn Juhl
finnjuhl.com

Poet sofa, 1941
Designed by Finn Juhl
— Page 160

Ikea
ikea.com

Äpplaryd sofa, 2021
Designed by
Maja Ganszyniec
— Page 120

Söderhamn sofa, 2010
Designed by Ola Wihlborg
— Page 138

Jot Jot
jotjot.com

Brick sofa, 2010
Designed by KiBiSi
— Page 014

Karimoku Case
karimoku-case.com

A-SO1 sofa, 2019
Designed by Keiji Ashizawa
& Norm Architects
— Page 112

La Cividina
lacividina.com

Osaka sofa, 1967
Designed by Pierre Paulin
— Page 052

Lisse sofa, 2025
Designed by Sabine Marcelis
— Page 042

Lema
lemamobili.com

Niveaux sofa, 2022
Designed by Federica Biasi
— Page 166

Living Divani
livingdivani.it

Extrasoft sofa, 2008
Designed by Piero Lissoni
— Page 056

Sumo sofa, 2020
Designed by Piero Lissoni
— Page 076

Louis Vuitton
louisvuitton.com

Big C sofa, 1969
Designed by Pierre Paulin
— Page 102

Maruni
maruni.com

Hiroshima sofa, 2009
*Designed by
Naoto Fukasawa*
— Page 074

Minotti
minotti.com

Horizonte sofa, 2022
Designed by Studio MK27
— Page 022

Moroso
moroso.it

Gentry sofa, 2011
*Designed by
Patricia Urquiola*
— Page 038

Sancal
sancal.com

Sax sofa, 2005
Designed by Rafa García
— Page 106

SCP
scp.co.uk

Peonia sofa, 2023
*Designed by
Wilkinson & Rivera*
— Page 178

Studio Nada Debs
nadadebs.com

Zen sofa, 2021
Designed by Nada Debs
— Page 066

Vitra
vitra.com

Anagram sofa, 2024
*Designed by
Panter&Tourron*
— Page 024

Polder sofa, 2005
Designed by Hella Jongerius
— Page 028

Slow sofa, 2025
*Designed by Ronan
& Erwan Bouroullec*
— Page 170

Woodmark
woodmark.com.cn

801 Series sofa, 2001
Designed by Charles Wilson
— Page 140

Youth Éditions
youtheditions.fr

Patrick sofa, 2024
Designed by Joris Poggioli
— Page 046

Bespoke sofas

Custom-made window
seat, 2022
Designed by Shim-Sutcliffe
— Page 032

Custom-upcycled sofa,
2024
Designed by Yinka Ilori
— Page 060

Custom-made sofa, 2005
*Designed by
Brooks + Scarpa*
— Page 084

Theatre sofa, 2022
Designed by Eric Owen Moss
— Page 098

Correa sofa, 1990
Designed by Charles Correa
— Page 124

Custom-made sofa, 2005
*Designed by Chatpong
Chuenrudeemol*
— Page 130

Siesta sofa, 2019
*Designed by
Fernanda Canales*
— Page 150

Custom-made sofa, 2021
Designed by Tamsin Johnson
— Page 156

Custom-made sofa, 2024
Designed by Joyce Wang
— Page 164

Index

5011 sofa 199
514 Refolo sofa 194, 202
620 sofa 204
801 Series sofa 140—143
&Tradition 200

A

A sofa 154—155
A-S01 sofa 7, 112—115
Aalto, Aino 189
Aalto, Alvar 189, 199
Aarnio, Eero 206
ABCD 3-seater sofa 206
Acerbis 45, 208
Adelta Oy 197
Agnoli, Tito 211
Aidan sofa 88—89
Airborne 204
Air Frame sofa 213
Albini, Franco 198,
    200—201
Alfredo Paredes Studio
    176
Alias 211
Allen, Davis 203
Alpha sofa 197
Anagram sofa 24—27
Andersen, Johannes 201
Andraos, Amale 28—31
Äpplaryd sofa 120—123
Arad, Ron 212
Archibong, Ini 7, 24—27,
    202
Archizoom Associati 190,
    195, 205—206
Arflex 7, 49—51, 201
Art deco sofa 198
Artek 199
Artifort 206
Ashizawa, Keiji 7,
    113—115
Atelier Jean Prouvé 203
L'Atelier Móveis 207
Audo Copenhagen 199
Azucena 209

B

B&B Italia 72—73, 190,
    207
Baker Furniture 201
Baker sofa 201

Barber Osgerby 72—73, 213
Barcelona couch 189
Bartoli, Carlo 209
Basket sofa 205
Batlló bench 196
Bauhaus sofa 198
BD Barcelona 144, 191, 196
Belladonna sofa 201
Bellini, Mario 144, 169,
    190, 195, 197, 207
Bench No 356 203
Bentwood sofa 196
Biasi, Federica 167—169
Big C sofa 103—105
Bilbao, Tatiana 7, 108—111
Bjarke Ingels Group (BIG)
    16—17
Blu Dot 180—183
Blue sofa 197
Boeri, Cini 129, 209
Boesen, Viggo 200
Bogo sofa 209
Bonacina 205
Botta, Mario 211
Bouroullec, Erwan
    96—97, 172—173
Bouroullec, Ronan
    96—97, 171—173
Bravo, Rodrigo 94—97
Brdr Krüger 136—137
Breuer, Marcel 193, 198,
    200
Breuer 2-Seater sofa 200
Brick sofa 7, 14—17
Brigadier sofa 209
Brooks, Angie 85—87
Bunshaft, Gordon 203
By Lassen 199

C

Califfo sofa 204
Camaleonda Modular sofa
    144, 169, 190, 207
Cameo Chair 86
Can sofa 94—97
Canales, Fernanda 7,
    151—153
Caon, David 10—13
Capitol Complex sofa 194,
    202
Cappellini 72, 213

Capri sofa 201
Carl Hansen & Son 149
Casas i Bardés 196
Cassina 12—13, 36, 190,
    196—198, 202, 206,
    208, 210, 213, 215
Castiglioni, Achille 13,
    210—211
CB2 128—129
Cecchi, Marzio 206
Chat Architects 132
Chen, Eran 56—59
Chesterfield sofa 17, 188
Chieftain sofa 201
Chipperfield, David 195,
    213
Chuenrudeemol, Chatpong
    7, 131—133
Citterio, Antonio
    110—111, 195, 213
ClassiCon 197
Cloud (studio) 44
Cloverleaf sofa 207
Club sofa 62—65
Collective 50—51
Colombo, Joe 13, 46, 205,
    213
Confidential sofa 208
Correa, Charles 124
Correa sofa 124—125
Couch 198
Coupé sofa 207
Cournet, Paul 42—45
Craft Associates 203
Crate & Barrel 88
Crawford, Ilse 80—83,
    211
Cube sofa 207

D

Dalí, Salvador 191
De Lucchi, Michele 195,
    210—211
De Padova 211
De Pas, D'Urbino &
    Lomazzi 209
De Sede 116—119, 208
Debs, Nada 66—69
DeJean, Joan 188
Devalle sofa 200
Diwan sofa 191

Djinn sofa 204
DMC Made 100
Dominioni, Luigi Caccia
    209
Double Soft Big Easy 212
Driade 210, 213
DS-80 daybed 116—119
DS-1025 Terrazza sofa 208
Ducaroy, Michel 190, 208
Dudet Bold sofa 36—37
Dudet sofa 215
Due Foglie sofa 203

E

Eames, Charles and Ray
    189, 194, 211
Ecart International 64
Edra 212
Eiermann, Egon 206
Elan sofa 7, 70—73
Er, Cherie 19—21
ES 108 Three-Seat sofa 211
Etel 210
Eva sofa 200
Extrasoft sofa 56—59

F

F51-3 sofa 197
Faleschini, Guido 207
Fauteuil Grand Confort
    189, 194, 197
FD147L sofa 146—149
Filo sofa 213
Firma Karl Mathsson 200
Fledermaus sofa 196
Flexform 7, 108—111, 213
Formel A 154
Foster, Norman 195, 214
Foster 620 bench 214
France & Daverkosen 148
Frank, Jean-Michel 62—65
Frankl, Paul T 199
Fredericia Furniture
    92—93, 207
Free System sofa 208
Fritz Hansen 203
Fukasawa, Naoto 72,
    74—75, 207

G

Galleria Colombari 200
Ganszyniec, Maja 122
García, Rafa 106
Gatti, Piero 206
Gaudí, Antoni 196
GE-290/3 sofa 202
Gehry, Frank 195, 213
Gehry sofa 213
Gentry sofa 39—41
George Smith 82—83
Getama 202
Gillon, Jean 205
Glade sofa 191
Goode, Sarah E 188
Gottwald, Hynek 198
Gray, Eileen 197
Gropius, Walter 193, 197
Groundpiece sofa 213
Gubi 205

H
H Pander & Zonen 198
Hadid, Zaha 195, 212
Hansen, Fritz 203
Hay 94—97
Heatherwick, Thomas 195, 215
Heinz & Co 196
Helg, Franca 201
Heller 213
Herman Miller 20—21, 138, 211, 214
Hildebrand, Thomas 116—119
Hiroshima sofa 74—75
Hoffmann, Josef 189, 193, 196—197
Holl, Steven 62—65
Hollein, Hans 191, 210
Honeta 206
Horizonte sofa 22—23
Hotz, Jeramie 10—13
House of Finn Juhl 162, 201
How High the Moon 211
Hvidt & Mølgaard 148—149

I
I4 Mariani 207
Idée 211

Ikea 44—45, 51, 82, 122—123, 138—39, 191
Ilori, Yinka 60—61
Ilse sofa 80—83
Industrial Facility 200, 214
Ingels, Bjarke 7, 14—17
In-side sofa 215
Isokon Plus 200
Issoufou, Mariam 126—129
Italma Woodart 205

J
J & J Kohn 196
Jackson Law 164
Jacobsen, Arne 194, 200, 203
Jeanneret, Pierre 189, 194, 197, 202
Johnson, Tamsin 156—159
Jongerius, Hella 30—31
Jot Jot 16
Jota sofa 90—93
Judd, Donald 191
Juhl, Finn 160—163, 194, 201

K
Kandissi sofa 209
Kar-a-Sutra 190
Karimoku Case 114—115
Karm sofa 7, 135—137
Kartell 213
KiBiSi 16—17
Kiesler, Friedrich 189, 200
Klint, Kaare 199
Klug, Ubald 208
Knole Settee 187—188, 191
Knoll, Florence 189, 194, 202
Knoll 72—73, 86, 189, 200, 202, 205, 209, 214
Kodai, Yuichi 76—79
Kogan, Marcio 22—23
Kubus sofa 189, 197
Kuramata, Shiro 211

L
La Cividina 44—45, 54—55

Lady sofa 201
Larsen, Sigurd 154—155
Lassen, Flemming 199
Le Corbusier 65, 105, 189, 193—194, 197
Lee, Olivia 138—139
Leeman, Walter 207
Lema 168—169
Libeskind, Daniel 7, 103—105
Lido sofa 210
Ligne Roset 172, 190, 208
Lisse sofa 42—45
Lissoni, Piero 58—59, 78
Little Petra VB2 sofa 200
Living Divani 58—59, 76—79
Lota sofa 197
Louis Vuitton 104—105
Luva sofa 19—21

M
Mad Chaise Longue 214
Mae West Lips sofa 191
Maggi, Claudia 76—79
Magis 93, 215
Magistretti, Vico 12—13, 144, 197, 208, 211
Major, Chris 7, 141—143
Malitte furniture 190
Malmsten, Carl 197
Mandrup, Dorte 160—163
Maralunga sofa 10—13, 144, 208
Marcelis, Sabine 42—45
Marcus-Bello, Nifemi 120—123
Marenco, Mario 50—51
Marenco sofa 7, 49—51
Marilyn sofa 191, 210
Mariposa sofa 73
Maritz, Anita 180—183
Maruni 74, 106
Mathsson, Bruno 194, 200
Matta, Roberto 190
Maxwell, Helen 146—149
Maxwell, Niall 146—149
Mazo 199
Mehrotra, Rahul 124—125
Memphis Group 195

Memphis Milano 210
Mendini, Alessandro 195, 209
Mermelada Estudio 128—129
Mies van der Rohe, Ludwig 105, 189—190, 193, 202, 205, 214
Minotti 22
Mobel Italia 206
Model No 263 sofa 205
Mogensen, Børge 207
Mollino, Carlo 200
Molteni&C 203
Momentum Textiles & Wallcovering 60
Moroso 39—41, 212
Morrison, Jasper 70, 72—73, 90—93, 106, 207
Moss, Eric Owen 99—101
Mourgue, Olivier 204
Moussavi, Farshid 52—55
Muller, Fien 144—145
Muller Van Severen 144
Mustonen, Alex 180—183

N
Nagayama, Yuko 106—107
Nakashima, George 203
Neutra, Richard 197
Ng, Betty 7, 49—51
Nielsen, Martin 135—137
Niemeyer, Oscar 210
Niveaux sofa 167—169
Nmbello Studio 123
Norm Architects 114—115

O
Obliqua sofa 211
OCA Meia-Pataca 204
ODA 58
Officina della Scala 198
ON sofa 210
Origin Made 20—21
Osaka sofa 52—55
Osgerby, Jay 7, 70—73, 202
Oshinowo, Tosin 88—89
Owens, Rick 191

Index

P

Panter&Tourron 26—27
Panton, Verner 194, 200, 203, 207
Paolini, Cesare 206
Paredes, Alfredo 174—177
Party Lounge sofa 189, 200
Patrick sofa 46—47
Paulin, Pierre 7, 46, 54—55, 103—105, 206
Pearsall, Adrian 194, 203
Peonia sofa 7, 178—179
Perriand, Charlotte 189, 194, 197, 202
Perron, Willo 191
Pesce, Gaetano 190—191, 195, 207, 210
Pillow sofa 144—145
Platform 2006-S sofa 203
Platner, Warren 194, 205
Platner sofa 205
Poet sofa 160—163
Poggioli, Joris 46—47
Polder sofa 28—31
Poliform 214
Poltrona Frau 211
Poltronova 204—206, 210
Ponti, Gio 197, 203, 211
Pretzel Rattan sofa 199
Prototype 65, 200
Prouvé, Jean 203

R

Radical Design 194
Raffles sofa 211
Rams, Dieter 204, 211
Récamier, Juliette 188
Relaxed sofa 189, 202
Rietveld, Gerrit 198
Rivera, Teresa 7, 178—179
RMA Architects 124
Robie 3 sofa 196
Rodeio sofa 205
Rodrigues, Sergio 204
Ronan & Erwan Bouroullec 96—97, 172
Rosenthal 206
Rosselli, Alberto 208
Rossi di Albizzate 209
Rud Rasmussen 199

Rural Office 148

S

Saarinen, Eero 189, 200, 202
Saarinen, Eliel 197
Sacco sofa 206
Safari sofa 190, 206
Salocchi, Claudio 208
Samsas sofa 197
Sancal 106
Sancarlo sofa 210
Santana sofa 174—177
Saporiti 208
Saratoga sofa 204
Sausage 191
Sax sofa 106—107
Scarpa, Afra 190, 206
Scarpa, Lawrence 85—87
Scarpa, Tobia 190, 206
SCP 178
Serpente sofa 206
Settebello sofa 209
Shim, Brigitte 32—35
Shim-Sutcliffe 34—35
Siesta sofa 7, 151—153
Sika Design 201
Silver Series sofa 206
Sjögren, O H 197
Slow sofa 171—173
Snarkitecture 182—183
Söderhamn sofa 138—139
Sofa/daybed 206
Soft Dream sofa 7, 108—111
Soriana sofa 190, 206
Sottsass, Ettore 195, 204
Starck, Philippe 195, 213
Stephensen, Magnus Læssøe 199
Strato sofa 126—129
Studio Alchimia 209
Studio MK27 22
Studio Most 206
Studioilse 82—83
Sumo sofa 76—79
Sunday sofa 180—183
Sunset in New York (see Tramonto a New York) 210
Superonda sofa 190, 205

Swan sofa 203

T

T33 sofa 198
Tacchini 210
Tan, Gabriel 19—21
Tank sofa 189, 199
Tecta 197—198
Teodoro, Franco 206
Terada Tekkojo 211
Theatre sofa 99—101
Thonet 196
Thonet Industries USA 203
Thulstrup, David 7, 135—137
TMBO sofa 199
Togo chair 27
Togo sofa 190, 208
Tokyo-Pop sofa 213
Tonico sofa 204
Toro sofa 209
Toscani, Oliviero 190
Tramonto a New York 191, 210
Trensums 201
Tsachrelia, Dimitra 62—65
Tucroma sofa 207
Tuxedo Loveseat sofa 203

U

Uncle Jack sofa 213
Up collection 190
Urquiola, Patricia 36—37, 40—41, 195, 197, 215
Utrecht sofa 198

V

Van Severen, Hannes 144—145
Vannini, Moreno 167—169
Vario Pillo sofa 206
Velda 207
Verpan 207
Vignelli, Lella 204
Vignelli, Massimo 204
Vilhelm sofa 199
Vitra 7, 26—27, 30—31, 44—45, 72—73, 93,

172—173
Vitsoe 204
Vodder, Niels 201
Vogtherr, Burkhard 206
VS 197

W

Wagner, Otto 193, 196
Wai, Hunn 138—139
Walse sofa 211
Walter Knoll 13, 214
Wanders, Marcel 31, 195, 214
Wang, Joyce 164—165
Wardle, John 39—41
Wave sofa 212
Wegner, Hans 149, 194, 202
Welsh, David 7, 141—143
Welsh + Major 142
West, Franz 191
Widdicomb sofa 203
Widdicomb-Mueller 203
Wiener Werkstätte 193
Wihlborg, Ola 138
Wilkinson, Grant 7, 178—179
Wilkinson & Rivera 178
Wilson, Charles 141—143
Wireframe sofa 214
Wittmann 197, 200
Womb sofa 189, 200
Wood, Dan 28—31
Woodmark 7, 142—143
WorkAC 30—31
Wright, Frank Lloyd 65, 196

Y

Yoshioka, Tokujin 213
Youth Éditions 46

Z

Zalszupin, Jorge 207
Zanotta 206, 209
Zanuso, Marco 195, 201
Zen sofa 66—69
Zeppelin sofa 207

About Monocle

In 2007, *Monocle* was launched as a monthly magazine briefing on global affairs, business, design and more. Today we have a thriving print business, a radio station, shops, cafés, books, films and events. At our core is the simple belief that there will always be a place for a brand that is committed to telling fresh stories, delivering good journalism and being on the ground around the world. We're Zürich and London-based and have bureaux in Hong Kong, Paris and Tokyo.
Subscribe at *monocle.com*.

Monocle Magazine
Monocle is published 10 times a year, including two double issues (July/August and December/January). We also have annual specials: *The Forecast*, *The Entrepreneurs*, *The Escapist* and *The Design Directory*. Look out for our seasonal newspapers too.

Monocle Radio
Our round-the-clock online radio station delivers global news and shows covering foreign affairs, urbanism, business, culture, food and drink, design and print media. You can listen live or download shows from *monocle.com/radio* – or wherever you get your podcasts.

Books
Since 2013, *Monocle* has been publishing books such as this one, covering a range of topics from travel guides and home design to how to live a gentler life. Our books are available through our distribution partner Thames & Hudson at all good bookshops or on our website at *monocle.com/shop/print*

Monocle Minute
Monocle's smartly appointed family of newsletters comes from our team of editors and bureau chiefs around the world. From the daily *Monocle Minute* to *The Monocle Weekend Editions* and our weekly *Monocle Minute On Design* special, sign up to get the latest in affairs, entrepreneurship and design, straight to your inbox every day – all for free.
monocle.com/minute.

Shops
Monocle cares about bricks and mortar. It's why we've established outposts far and wide – you can find us in London, Paris, Zürich, Merano, Toronto, Tokyo and Hong Kong (and should you be jet-setting, Frankfurt and Hong Kong International airports too) – where wall-to-wall offerings of fine international threads, peppy print and smart stationery are on sale, designed in-house and by the brands we most admire. To step inside our shop is to step inside our pages.
monocle.com/shop

Cafés
Whether you are in the mood for the perfect flat white, a delicious sandwich or an evening aperitif, the friendly staff at our cafés have you covered. All our selections pair beautifully with the latest issue of the magazine – pop in for a chat, should you find yourself on London's Chiltern Street, Zürich's Dufourstrasse or Rue Bachaumont in Paris.
monocle.com/monocle-shops-and-cafe

Acknowledgments

Monocle

Editorial Director & Chairman
Tyler Brûlé

Editor in Chief
Andrew Tuck

Creative Director
Richard Spencer Powell

Production Director
Jacqueline Deacon

Photography Director
Matthew Beaman

Art Director
Sam Brogan

Monocle Book of Designers on Sofas

Head of Book Publishing
Virginia McLeod

Editors
Nic Monisse and
Virginia McLeod

Designer
Sam Brogan

Photography Editor
Sara Taglioretti

Production Coordinator
Marta Fernàndez Canut

Sub Editor
Matt Dupuy

Picture Researcher
Sarah Bell

Writers
Virgiliu Andone
Anindito Ariwandono
Desi Bandli
Grace Charlton
Gabriele Dellisanti
Naomi Xu Elegant
Mary Holland
Jane Horton
Claudia Jacob
Julia Jenne
Rory Jones
Joseph Koh
Tomos Lewis
Sam Lubell
Fiona Ma
Millie McArthur
Callum McDermott
Lucrezia Motta
Justin Quirk
Prasad Ramamurthy
Alex Rayner
Carlota Rebelo
Henry Rees-Sheridan
Stella Roos
Annick Weber
Fiona Wilson

Cover Illustrator
Karin Kellner

Photographers
Declan Blackall
Timothee Chambovet
Derek Delahunt
Mathias Eis
Kevin Faingnaert
Peyton Fulford
Yoshitsugu Fuminari
Cleo Goossens
Sabine Hess
Annika Kafcaloudis
Asuka Ito
Francesca Jones
Guo Jie Khoo
Keerthana Kunnath
Lit Ma
Benjamin Malapris
Cristobal Marambio
Meghan Marin
Benjamin McMahon
Alessandro Mitola
Zed Nelson
Anna Nielsen
Nana Yaw Oduro
Felipe Redondo
Stefan Ruiz
Miki Frances Sankhara
Samuel Schalch
Natthawut Taeja
Caroline Tompkins
Matilde Viegas
Paola Vivas
Dan Wilton
Jagoda Wisniewska

ISBN 978-0-500-96642-6

55000